CZECH

DICTIONARY & PHRASEBOOK

CZECH-ENGLISH • ENGLISH-CZECH

CW00953990

Dictionary & Phrasebooks

Albanian	Japanese *Romanized*
Arabic (Eastern) *Romanized*	Lao *Romanized*
Australian	Lingala
Azerbaijani	Malagasy
Basque	Maltese
Bosnian	Mongolian
Breton	Nepali
British	Norwegian
Cajun French	Pilipino (Tagalog)
Chechen	Polish
Croatian	Québécois
Czech	Romanian
Danish	Romansch
Esperanto	Russian
Estonian	Shona
Finnish	Slovak
French	Somali
Georgian	Spanish (Latin American)
German	Swahili
Greek	Swedish
Hebrew	Tajik
Hungarian	Thai *Romanized*
Igbo	Turkish
Ilocano	Ukrainian
Irish	Uzbek
Italian	

CZECH

DICTIONARY & PHRASEBOOK

CZECH-ENGLISH • ENGLISH-CZECH

Michaela Burilkovová

HIPPOCRENE BOOKS, INC.
New York

© 2003 Michaela Burilkovová

All rights reserved.

ISBN 0-7818-0942-8

For information, address:
Hippocrene Books, Inc.
171 Madison Avenue
New York, NY 10016

Cataloging-in-Publication data available from the Library of Congress.

Printed in the United States of America.

Many thanks to my family.

— M. Burilkovová

CONTENTS

INTRODUCTION

The Czech Republic is made up of three parts: Bohemia, Moravia and a part of Silesia. Located in the heart of Europe, the Czech lands have seen many turns in their history, which spans more than 2000 years. They were settled first by Celtic, later by German, and then by Slavic tribes. Two major historical regions emerged: Bohemia and Moravia. These regions existed with varying degrees of interdependence for more than one thousand years, before they came together with Slovakia to form the modern Czechoslovak state in 1918.

The Czech language, sometimes also called Bohemian, is a member of the West Slavic group from the family of Slavic languages, which is part of the great Indo-European family of languages.

From around the sixth century A.D., Slavic tribes were moving into the Slovak and Moravian lands and also into Bohemia from the southeast. In the seventh century the Slavic tribes migrating from North to Central Europe were united by Samo in the "Empire." This was the first Western Slavic political formation, but it did not survive after Samo's death.

The founder and first known ruler of the Great Moravian Empire was Mojmír I (in the ninth century). After him came the priest Rostislav, who in 862 appealed to the Byzantine emperor Michael III for a Christian mission. Michael sent the brothers Constantine (who later took the monastic name Cyril) and Methodius. They arrived in Moravia in 863 and began spreading Eastern Orthodox Christianity.

Constantine invented an alphabet (glagolitic) based on the Greek alphabet and the Slavic dialect in the region of Thessaloniki. He and his brother translated the Bible into this "Old Church Slavonic" language. Around the tenth century, due to the influence of Roman Catholicism, the Latin alphabet was adopted by the inhabitants of the Czech lands. The Great Moravian Empire disintegrated with the invasion of the Magyars early in the tenth century.

The end of the ninth century saw the birth of the Bohemian Czech state under Prince Bořivoj, the first historically documented member of the Přemyslid dynasty.

In 1085 Prince Vratislav II was crowned as the Czech king. He was the first king of Bohemia.

A document called the *Golden Bull of Sicily*, written in 1212, revised the relation of the Czech state to the Holy Roman Empire. The Bohemian rulers were now kings by inheritance and the kingdom became a recognized part of the Holy Roman Empire. In addition, the Bohemian king gained the right to be one of the seven electors of the Holy Roman Emperor.

During the 13th century the typical Gothic style of architecture emerged in the Czech lands.

Charles IV (Karel, originally named Václav) (lived 1316–1378) was the first Bohemian ruler to ascend to the throne with the Pope's support, in 1346. In Rome in 1355 he was crowned Holy Roman Emperor, thus becoming the head of all Western Christianity. In 1348

Charles IV founded Charles University in Prague, the first university in Central Europe. He built the Castle Karlštejn and a famous bridge in Prague (now called Charles Bridge) in the Gothic style. He also founded Prague's New Town. During this time, known as the Golden Age, the Czech lands reached the height of their economic and cultural development.

Master Jan Hus (1371–1415) was a chancellor at the University of Prague. After 1402 he was a preacher in Bethlehem Chapel in the Old Town of Prague. Around this time he wrote a paper *De orthographia Bohemica* (On the Czech orthography), where he presented a basic simplified spelling for the Czech language. Hus was influenced by the ideas of the English religious reformer John Wycliff. In several papers including *De ecclesia* (On the Church, 1413), he explained his approach to Church reforms. In 1415 he was burned as a heretic by Church officials after an inquisition-like process. However, his ideas became very popular among the Czech people. The mounting tension between Catholics and Hussites culminated in the Hussite revolution (1419–1436), led by Jan Žiška.

In 1526 the Catholic Hapsburgs came to the Czech throne, as Kings of Bohemia. There was a power struggle between the Hapsburg monarchs and the Bohemian Estates (Czech nationals, many of whom were Hussites). In 1620, the Bohemians were decisively defeated by the Hapsburgs at the Battle of White Mountain. This led to a period of re-Catholicization. The Czech state was declared a part of the Hapsburg (Austro-Hungarian) empire, and the Czech language and culture were suppressed.

During the seventeenth and eighteenth centuries the Czech Baroque style emerged. Many townhouses and villages were built in this style.

In 1781, the Edict of Toleration established freedom of religion. The Lutheran, Calvinist, and Orthodox confessions were legalized. The end of the eighteenth century and most of the nineteenth century was characterized by the beginning of the Czech National Revival. This included increasing the importance of the Czech language, which was in danger of losing ground to the German language, and building the Czech national culture. These times were marked by such famous figures as the composers Dvořák and Smetana, as well as the painter Mucha, to name just a few. The cultural emancipation of this period laid the foundations for the political independence of the Czechs. Around 1900 the *Secese* or Art Nouveau style emerged.

In October 1918, a new state—Czechoslovakia— was formed after the dissolution of Austria-Hungary. T. G. Masaryk was the first president.

In 1939, Bohemia and Moravia were occupied by Nazi Germany. The liberation of Czechoslovakia came in May 1945, after the Prague Uprising and the advance of Russia's Red Army. In 1948, the Communist party consolidated its grip on power, thus starting a forty-one-year period of totalitarian rule. January 1968 marked the beginning of the "Prague Spring," an attempt to introduce "socialism with a human face," which ended abruptly with the invasion of the Warsaw Pact armies later the same year.

In 1989, the "Velvet Revolution" brought about the fall of Communism. In the same year, the dissident Václav Havel became president of the Republic of Czechoslovakia.

In 1993 two new states were formed: the Czech Republic and the Slovak Republic.

ABBREVIATIONS

1.	1st person
2.	2nd person
3.	3rd person
adj.	adjective
adv.	adverb
conj.	conjunction
F	feminine
gram.	grammatical
imperf.	imperfect (for verbs)
interj.	interjection
M	masculine
Ma	masculine animate
Mi	masculine inanimate
N	neuter
n.	noun
num.	number
p.	case (in Czech, **pád**)
part.	particle
perf.	perfect (for verbs)
pl.	plural
prep.	preposition
pron.	pronoun
sg.	singular
v.	verb

THE CZECH ALPHABET

Czech Letter	Pronunciation — English equivalent sounds for Czech letter
A	[a]
B	[be]
C	[tse]
Č	[che]
D	[de]
Ď, ď	[dye]
E	[e]
F	[ef]
G	[ge]
H	[ha]
CH	[Ha]
I	[ee]
J	[ye]
K	[ka]
L	[el]
M	[em]
N	[en]
Ň	[enye]
O	[aw]
P	[pe]
Q	[kve]
R	[er]
Ř	[erj]
S	[es]
Š	[esh]
T	[te]
Ť, ť	[tye]
U	[oo]
ú, ů	[oo]
V	[ve]

W	[dvo-yite ve]
X	[iks]
Y	[ipsilon]
Z	[zet]
Ž	[jet]

PRONUNCIATION GUIDE

a	**u** as in **u**p
á	**a** as in f**a**ther
aj	**i** as in p**i**ne
au	**ou** as in **ou**t
b	**b** as in **b**ank
c	**ts** as in ca**ts**
č	**ch** as in **ch**eese
d	**d** as in **d**ime
ď	a very slight **dy** sound
dž	**j** as in **j**am
e	**e** as in s**e**t
é	**e** but longer, something like the a in c**a**re
ě	**ye** as in **ye**t
ej	**a** as in **a**pe
f	same as in English
g	**g** as in **g**ood
h	**h** as in **h**and
ch	**ch** as in Ba**ch**
i	**i** as in p**i**t
í	**ee** as in f**ee**l
j	**y** as in **y**es
k	same as in English
l	same as in English
m	same as in English
n	same as in English
ň	**y** after **n**, like **ny** in ca**ny**on
o	**o** as in n**o**t
ó	**a** as in c**a**ll
oj	**oy** as in b**oy**
ou	**o** as in g**o**
p	same as in English
q	**qu** as in **qu**ack
r	**r** as in **r**olling

ř	close to **rzh** (pronounced soft **r** with **ž**), there is no equivalent in English
s	same as in English
š	**sh** as in **sh**ell
t	same as in English
ť	slight **ty** sound, as **tu** in **tu**lip (British)
u	**u** as in p**u**t
ú, ů	**oo** as in t**oo**l
v	same as in English
w	**v** as in **v**isit
y	**i** as in **i**s
ý	**ee** as in f**ee**l
z	**z** as in **z**ebra
ž	**s** as in plea**s**ure

1) In Czech, the stress is always on the first syllable of the word.

2) When a preposition appears before a noun, stress is on the preposition.

3) e (or é) at the end of a Czech word is always pronounced.

4) The Czech word **mě** is pronounced **mně**.

Czech spelling is more phonetic than English, but it has developed some characteristic features.

There are five vowels in Czech:

short – **a, e, i, o, u**
long – **á, é, í, ó, ú, ů**
diphthongs – **ou** – nes**ou** (they carry)
              au – **au**to (car)
              eu – pn**eu**matika (tire)

Czech consonants have different phonetic pronunciations:

voiced – **b, v, d, ď, z, ž, g, h, m, n, ň, ř; l, r, j**
(their articulation is accompanied by vibration of the vocal chords)
voiceless – **p, f, t, ť, s, š, k, ch, c, č** (after pronunciation the vocal chords do not vibrate)

The voiced-voiceless consonant pairs: voiced consonants are pronounced as their voiceless counterparts at the end of words (the spelling remains the same).

b > [p]	klu**b** (club)
v > [f]	kre**v** (blood)
d > [t]	le**d** (ice)
z > [s]	obra**z** (picture)
ž > [š]	nů**ž** (knife)
ď > [ť]	lo**ď** (boot)
g > [k]	geolo**g** (geologist)
h > [ch]	sní**h** (snow)

Consonants are also:

hard – **h, g, ch, k, r, d, t, n,** (velar) – after them you write - **y/ý**
soft – **ž, š, c, č, ř, ď, ť, ň, j** (palatal) – after them you write – **i/í**
ambiguous - either hard or soft – **b, f, m, p, s, v, z** – after them you write either – **y/ý** or - **i/í**, depending on the etymology of the word.

The difference between hard and soft consonants is very important for the cases in Czech grammar: the declension of nouns depends on them, resulting in hard or soft models of declension.

Some examples of syllables:

hard: da, ta, na
do, to, no
du, tu, nu
de, te, ne
dy, ty, ny
dý, tý, ný

soft: ďa, ťa, ňa
ďo, ťo, ňo
ďu, ťu, ňu
dě, tě, ně
di, ti, ni
dí, tí, ní

ambiguous: by - bi   **by**t (flat)
biologie (biology),
bílý (white)
fy - fi   **fy**zika (physics)
filologie (philology)
py – pi   **py**žamo (pyjamas)
pivo (beer),
píseň (song)

A BASIC CZECH GRAMMAR

NOUNS

Czech nouns have no articles before them. Grammatically they are masculine, feminine, and neuter (abbreviated M, F, N). They denote the names of persons – **člověk** (human being), **muž** (man), **žena** (woman), **dítě** (child), of animals – **pes** (dog), **kočka** (cat), of things – **mrak** (cloud), **čepice** (cap), of actions – **písknutí** (whistling), and quality – **důvěřivost** (credulity). Most words denoting human beings are feminine or masculine according to the sex. Words denoting children or young animals are neuter. Names of plants, animals or things can be of any gender. Furthermore, the masculine nouns in the Czech language are divided in two principal groups: animate, for living things – **muž** (man), (abbreviation **Ma**), and inanimate, for all other nouns – **stroj**, **stůl** (machine, table), (abbreviation **Mi**). The Ma and Mi nouns sometimes have different forms (see the discussion on adjectives, syntax, and cases).

For example:
- Ma – **student, muž** (student, man)
- Mi – **čaj, dopis** (tea, letter)
- F – **přítelkyně, žena** (girlfriend, woman)
- N – **moře, dítě** (sea, child)

Masculine and Feminine

Some feminine nouns have different forms than their masculine counterparts. Most masculine nouns end in consonants – hard or soft: **otec** (father), **kamarád** (friend). Most feminine nouns end in **-a** or in **-e,** or in soft consonants: **žena** (woman), **matka** (mother), **učebnice** (textbook), **loď** (ship).

Ma	Mi	F
muž (man)	**sešit** (notebook)	**žena** (woman)
chlapec (boy)	**stůl** (chair)	**dívka** (girl)

Quite often the feminine nouns are formed from the masculine by adding the suffix **-ka**.

Ma	F
student (student)	**studentka**
cizinec (foreigner)	**cizinka**

In some nouns hard consonants change into the corresponding soft consonants with the shift from the masculine to the feminine form.

M	F
Čech (Czech)	**Češka**
biolog (biologist)	**bioložka**

Neuter

Most neuter nouns end in **-o, -e** or **-í**: **jídlo** (food), **díte** (child), **štěstí** (happiness).

Singular and Plural

In Czech as in English, nouns are singular and plural. In English for regular nouns there is only one ending to denote the plural: **-s**. In Czech there are several endings. Czech has soft and hard plural endings for nouns.

Hard -y; -a

Mi

sg.	pl.
oblek (suit)	**obleky** (suits)
film (movie)	**filmy** (movies)

F

sg.	pl.
lampa (lamp)	**lampy** (lamps)
kniha (book)	**knihy** (books)

N

sg.	pl.
auto (car)	**auta** (cars)
radio (radio)	**radia** (radios)

Soft -e; -i

Mi

sg.	pl.
nápoj (beverage)	**nápoje** (beverages)
talíř (dish)	**talíře** (dishes)

F

sg.	pl.
sg.=pl. **učebnice** (textbook)	
skříň (wardrobe)	**skříně** (wardrobes)
věc (thing)	**věci** (things)

N

sg./pl.
sg.=pl. **vejce** (eggs)
sg.=pl. **pole** (fields)

As previously mentioned, masculine nouns denoting living things are called animate (**Ma**), and all other masculine nouns are called inanimate

(**Mi**). Masculine animate nouns take the plural endings **-i**, **-ové** or **-é**.

<u>Ma sg.</u>	<u>Ma pl.</u>
bratr (brother)	**bratři** (brothers)
otec (father)	**otcové** (fathers)

POSSESSIVE PRONOUNS

	<u>M</u>	<u>F</u>	<u>N</u>
sg.			
1. my	**můj**	**má**	**mé**
2. your	**tvůj**	**tvá**	**tvé**
3. his	**jeho**	**jeho**	**jeho**
her	**její**	**její**	**její**
pl.			
1. our	**náš**	**naše**	**naše**
2. your	**váš**	**vaše**	**vaše**
3. their	**jejich**	**jejich**	**jejich**

INTERROGATIVE PRONOUNS

Czech has two different interrogative pronouns.

sg. **Jaký, -á, -é**   Asking about the quality (what kind of, what sort of, what is).

pl. Ma **Jačí**   Mi, F **Jaké**   N **Jaká**

M	**Jaký je dnes den?**	What day is today?
F	**Jaká je Vaše velikost?**	What is your size?
N	**Jaké číslo máte?**	What is your number?

sg. **Který, -á, -é** Asking for a selection from a
group (which, what).

pl. Ma **Kteří**   Mi, F **Které**   N **Která**

M	**Který vlak jede dnes?**	Which train is leaving today?
F	**Která stanice je to?**	Which station is that?
N	**Které auto je naše?**	Which car is ours?

VERBS

Present Tense

Infinitive: to carry - v. **nést** (regular verb)

sg.	pl.
1. **nesu**	1. **neseme**
I am carrying	we are carrying
2. **neseš**	2. **nesete**
you are carrying	you are carrying
3. **nese**	3. **nesou**
he, she, it is carrying	they are carrying

negation: 1.sg. **nenesu** I am not carrying

Infinitive: to be - v. **být** (irregular verb)

sg.		pl.	
1. I am	**já jsem**	1. we are	**my jsme**
2. you are	**ty jsi**	2. you are	**vy jste**
3. he is	**on je**	3. they are	**oni jsou**
she is	**ona je**		
it is	**to(ono) je**		

Pronunciation: **jsem** [sem] I am

| (já) | **Jsem Američan.** | I am American. |
| (my) | **Jsme tady.** | We are here. |

Personal pronouns are not obligatory, as in English.
For the negative form, add the prefix **ne-** to the verb.

sg.		pl.	
1. I am not	**nejsem**	1. we are not	**nejsme**
2. you are not	**nejsi**	2. you are not	**nejste**
3. he is not	**není**	3. they are not	**nejsou**
she is not	**není**		
it is not	**není**		

Pronunciation: **nejsem** [nej-sem] I am not

Jan není doma.	John is not at home.
Není tady Eva?	Isn't Eva here?

Infinitive: to have - v. **mít**

sg.		pl.	
1. I have	**mám**	1. we have	**máme**
2. you have	**máš**	2. you have	**mate**
3. he has	**má**	3. they have	**mají**
she has	**má**		
it has	**má**		

Mám tužku.	I have a pencil.
Máte učebnice?	Do you have a textbook?
Máš propisku?	Do you have a pen?

Negation:

sg.		pl.	
1. I don't have	**nemám**	1. we don't have	**nemáme**
2. you don't have	**nemáš**	2. you don't have	**nemáte**
3. he doesn't have	**nemá**	3. they don't have	**nemají**
she doesn't have	**nemá**		
it doesn't have	**nemá**		

Nemám kapesník. I don't have a handkerchief.

Verb Tenses of v. **být** (to be) and v. **mít** (to have)

I am	1.sg. **/já/ jsem**	Present Tense
I was	1.sg. **byl/a jsem**	Past Tense (M/F)
I will be, I shall be	1.sg. **budu**	Future Tense

I have	1.sg. **mám**	Present Tense
I had	1.sg. **měl/a jsem**	Past Tense (M/F)
I will have	1.sg. **budu mít**	Future Tense

Past Tense

The past tense in Czech is always formed using the past participle of the verb followed by the present tense (in the appropriate person) of the verb **být** (to be). In the third person singular and plural the present tense form of **být** is omitted.

The past participle is formed by replacing the final **-t** of the infinitive with **-l, -la, -lo** (for sg. M, F, N) and **-li, -ly, -la** (for pl. Ma, Mi/F, N). It is called the *l-form*.

Forms of v. **být** (to be)

sg.		pl.	
1. **byl/a jsem**	I was	1. **byli/y jsme**	we were
2. **byl/a jsi**	you were	2. **byli/y jste**	you were
3. **byl/a/o**	he, she, it was	3. **byli/y/a**	they were

negation: 1.sg. **nebyl/a jsem** etc. I was not

Forms of v. **mít** (to have)

sg.		pl.	
1. **měl/a jsem**	I had	1. **měli/y jsme**	we had
2. **měl/a jsi**	you had	2. **měli/y jste**	you had
3. **měl/a/o**	he, she, it had	3. **měli/y**	they had

negation: 1.sg. **neměl/a jsem** etc. I had not

The Conditional

In Czech there are two types of conditional.

The conditional present tense of v. **být** (to be)

sg.		pl.	
1. **bych**	I would	1. **bychom**	we would
2. **bys**	you would	2. **byste**	you would
3. **by**	he, she, it would	3. **by**	they would

I would like	1. sg. **chtěl/a bych**
I would have to (+infinitive)	1. sg **musel/a bych**

sg.	pl.
1. **musel/a bych**	1. **museli/y bychom**
2. **musel/a bys**	2. **museli/y byste**
3. **musel/a/o by**	3. **museli/y by**

Negative form of conditional present tense: 1.sg. **nemusel/a bych** I wouldn't have to (+ infinitive)

sg.	pl.
nemusel/a bych	1. **nemuseli/y bychom**
nemusel/a bys	2. **nemuseli/y byste**
nemusel/a/o by	3. **nemuseli/y by**

The conditional past tense

Would be or I would have (+ past participle)
1.sg **byl bych** etc.
I should (+ infinitive) or I ought to (+ infinitive)
1.sg **měl bych** etc.

Negative form of the conditional past tense:
1.sg. **nebyl bych** etc
1.sg. **neměl bych** etc.

The Imperative

In Czech there are two types of imperative: short and long. The long imperative has an additional syllable in the ending. The plural form with the ending **-te** (mluvte) is for addressing several persons or one person in a polite way; the form with **-me** (mluvme) is "let us …".

The short imperative

	sg. 2nd person	pl. 2nd person	pl. 1st person
drink -	**pij**	**pijte**	**pijme**
wait -	**čekej**	**čekejte**	**čekejme**

Negative short imperative form

	sg. 2.	pl. 2.	pl. 1.
Do not drink	**nepij**	**nepijte**	**nepijme**
Do not wait	**nečekej**	**nečekejte**	**nečekejme**

The long imperative

	sg. 2.	pl. 2.	pl. 1.
read -	**čti**	**čtěte**	**čtěme**
sleep -	**spi**	**spěte**	**spěme**

Negative long imperative form

	sg. 2	pl.2.	pl.1.
Do not read	**nečti**	**nečtěte**	**nečtěme**
Do not sleep	**nespi**	**nespěte**	**nespěme**

v. **být** (to be) has an irregular imperative form:

	sg.	pl. 2.	pl. 1.
to be	**buď**	**buďte**	**buďme**
negation:			
not to be	**nebuď**	**nebuďte**	**nebuďme**

Poď jsem.	Come here.
Poďme na oběd.	Let us go for lunch.
Mluvme jenom česky.	Let us speak only Czech.

Verbs with reflexive pronouns

In Czech many verbs are accompanied by the reflexive pronouns **se** or **si**. Many of them (see examples below) convey no particular meaning and are merely traditional. Sometimes these verbs are truly reflexive and express actions performed by the subject upon him/herself. And sometimes they express reciprocity (like *each other* or *one another*).

to look, to watch	**dívat se**
to wish	**přát si**
to wash myself	**mýt se**
to know each other	**znát se**

v. **ptát se** (to ask - in present tense)
sg.

1. **ptám se**	I am asking
2. **ptáš se**	You are asking
3. **ptá se**	he, she, it is asking

pl.
1. **ptáme se**   we are asking
2. **ptáte se**   you are asking
3. **ptají se**   they are asking

negation: 1.sg. **neptám se** (I am not asking)

I am asking	1.sg. **Já se ptám** etc.	present tense
I asked	1.sg. **Ptal/a jsem se**	past tense
I will ask	1.sg. **Budu se ptát**	future tense
I would ask	1.sg. **Ptal/a bych se**	conditional present tense
I would have asked or I could have asked	1.sg. **Byl bych se ptal**	conditional past tense
Ask!	2.sg. **Ptej se!**	imperative

Ptám se učitele. I am asking the teacher.

Modal verbs

Present Tense

I want	1.sg. **chci**
I can, I am able to	1.sg. **můžu**
I must, I have to	1.sg. **musím**
I may, I am allowed to	1.sg. **smím**
I can, I know how to	1.sg. **umím/=dovedu/**
	1.sg. **dovedu**

Past Tense

1.sg. **chtěl/a jsem**	I wanted
1.sg. **mohl/a jsem**	I could
1.sg. **musel/a jsem**	I had to
1.sg. **směl/a jsem**	I might
1.sg. **uměl/a jsem**	I knew
1.sg. **dovedl/a jsem**	I could

v. **chtít** (to want - in present tense)

sg.	pl.
1. **chci** I want	1. **chceme** we want
2. **chceš** you want	2. **chcete** you want
3. **chce** he, she, it wants	3. **chtějí** they want

v. **chtít** (to want - in past tense)

sg.	pl.
1. **chtěl/a jsem** I wanted	1. **chtěli/y jsme** we wanted
2. **chtěl/a jsi** you wanted	2. **chtěli/y jste** you wanted
3. **chtěl/a/o** he, she, it wanted	3. **chtěli/y** they wanted

Negation:

Present Tense

I don't want	1.sg. **nechci**
I cannot	1.sg. **nemůžu**
I don't have to	1.sg. **nemusím**
I must not, I have not been allowed	1.sg. **nesmím**
I do not know	1.sg. **neumím**
I cannot	1.sg. **nedovedu**

Past Tense

I didn't want	1.sg. **nechtěl/a jsem**
I couldn't have, I couldn't	1.sg. **nemohl/a jsem**
I didn't have to	1.sg. **nemusel/a jsem**
I might not	1.sg. **nesměl/a jsem**
I did not know	1.sg. **neuměl/a jsem**
I could not	1.sg. **nedovedl/a jsem**

We must not be late. **Nesmíme přijít pozdě.**

Future Tense

Future Tense of **modal verbs**

I will want	1.sg. **budu chtít**
I will be able to	1.sg. **budu moci**
I will have to	1.sg. **budu muset**
I will be allowed	1.sg. **budu smět**
I will know	1.sg. **budu umět**

negation:

I will not want	1.sg. **nebudu chtít**
I will not be able to	1.sg. **nebudu moci**
I will not have to	1.sg. **nebudu muset**
I will not be allowed	1.sg. **nebudu smět**
I will not know	1.sg. **nebudu umět**

Future tense of v. **být** (to be)

sg.

1. **budu**	I shall be, I will be
2. **budeš**	you will be
3. **bude**	he, she, it will be

pl.

1. **budeme**	we shall be, we will be
2. **budete**	you will be
3. **budou**	they will be

negation: 1.sg. **nebudu** etc.

Future forms of v. **mít** (to have)

sg.

1.sg. **budu mít**	I will have
2.sg. **budeš mít**	you will have
3.sg. **bude mít**	he, she, it will have

pl.

1.pl. **budeme mít**	we will have
2.pl. **budete mít**	you will have
3.pl. **budou mít**	they will have

negation: 1.sg. **nebudu mít** etc.

Verbal aspect - imperfect and perfect

The imperfect verbs (abbreviation **imperf.**) express an action that is, was, or will be in existence, without limitation in time. The English equivalents are the present and past continuous tenses as well as the future tense using "will be." This aspect can indicate future, present, or past. Here are some examples: **Stát** (to stand): 1.sg. **stojím** (I am standing) present tense, 1.sg. **stál/a jsem** (I was standing) past tense, and 1.sg. **budu stát** (I will be standing) future tense. **Doufat** (to hope): 1.sg. **doufám** (I am hoping) present tense, 1.sg. **doufal/a jsem** (I was hoping) past tense, 1.sg. **budu doufat** (I will be hoping) future tense. **Házet** (to throw): 1.sg. **házím** (I am throwing) present tense, 1.sg. **hazel/a jsem** (I was throwing) past tense, and 1.sg. **budu házet** (I will be throwing) future tense.

The perfect verbs (abbreviation **perf.**) cannot express the present and correspond to the English perfect tenses. They represent an action that is limited in time. Their present form expresses the future and they also have past forms. Here are some examples: **zatočit se** (to turn around): 1.sg. **zatočím se** (I will turn around) future tense, 1.sg. **zatočil/a jsem se** (I have turned around) past tense, **chytnout** (to catch) 1.sg. **chutnu** (I will catch) future tense, 1.sg.**chytil/a jsem** (I have caught) past tense.

Perfect verbs are often formed by adding prefixes to imperfect verbs.

imperfect (imperf.)		perfect (perf.)
v. platit (to pay)	>	v. **za**platit
v. ptát se (to ask)	>	v. **ze**ptat se
v. dělat (to make)	>	v. **u**dělat
v. pít (to drink)	>	v. **vy**pít

Future Tense of imperfect and perfect verbs

The future tense of imperfect verbs is a two-word form: **budu** + infinitive. The future tense of perfect verbs has the same endings as the present tense.

v. imperf. **mluvit** (to speak).
1.sg. **budu mluvit**   I would speak
negation: 1.sg. **nebudu mluvit** I would not speak

v. imperf. **jít** (to go), add prefix **po-**
1.sg. **po**jedu perf.   I will go
negation: 1.sg. **nepojedu** I will not go

Examples of future and past tense:

v. imperf. **trávit** (to spend)
I was spending 1.sg. **trávil jsem** *l-form* past tense.
v. perf. **strávit**
I have spent   1.sg. **strávil jsem** *l-form* past tense
I will spend   1.sg. **strávím**   future
negation: I will not spend 1.sg. **nestrávím**

v. imperf **navštěvovat** (to visit)
I was visiting   1.sg. **navštěvoval jsem** *l-form*
                 past tense

v. perf. **navštívit**
I have visited   1.sg. **navštívil jsem** *l-form*
                  past tense
I will visit   1.sg. **navštívím** future
negation: I will not visit 1.sg. **nenavštívím**

Classification of Verbs

The Czech language has five classes of verbs distinguished by the ending in the third person singular of the present tense.

The first class of verbs
This class includes the verbs ending in **-e** in the 3.sg. (third person singular) in the present tense, when there is no **-n** or **-j** before the **-e**.

Infinitive
v. **nést** (to bring, to carry)
v. **brát** (to get, to take)
v. **mazat** (to grease)
v. **péci** (to fry)

Present tense in 3.sg.
nese (he, she, it is bringing)
bere (he, she, it is getting)
maže (he, she, it is greasing)
peče (he, she, it is frying)

Past tense in 3.sg.
nesl (he, she, it was bringing)
bral (he, she, it was taking)
mazal (he, she, it was greasing)
pecl (he, she, it was frying)

The second class of verbs
This class includes the verbs that end in **-ne** in the 3.sg. present tense.

Infinitive
v. **tisknuot** (to print)
v. **minout** (to miss, to pass)
v. **začít** (to begin)

Present tense in 3.sg.
tiskne (he, she, it is printing)
mine (he, she, it is passing)
začne (he, she, it is beginning)

Past tense in 3.sg.
tiskl (he, she, it was printing)
minul (he, she, it was missing)
začal (he, she, it was beginning)

The third class of verbs
This class includes the verbs that end in **-je** in the 3.sg. present tense.

Infinitive
v. **krýt** (to cover)
v. **kupovat** (to buy)

Present tense in 3.sg.
kryje (he, she, it is covering)
kupuje (he, she, it is buying)

Past tense in 3.sg.
kryl (he, she, it was covering)
kupoval (he, she, it was buying)

The fourth class of verbs
This class includes the verbs that end in **-í** in the 3.sg. present tense.

Infinitive
v. **prosit** (to pray)
v. **trpět** (to suffer)
v. **sázet** (to plant)

Present tense in 3.sg.
prosí (he, she, it is praying)
trpí (he, she, it is suffering)
sází (he, she, it is planting)

Past tense in 3.sg.
prosil (he, she, it was praying)
trpěl (he, she, it was suffering)
sázel (he, she, it was planting)

The fifth class of verbs
This class includes the verbs that end in **-á** in the 3.sg. present tense.

Infinitive
v. **dělat** (to make)

Present tense in 3.sg.
dělá (he, she, it is making)

Past tense in 3.sg.
dělal (he, she, it was making)

ADJECTIVES

Czech adjectives are of two types: "hard" or "soft." They agree in gender, number, and case with the nouns they qualify.

Hard adjectives end differently according to gender: for M sg. they end in **-ý,** for F sg. in **-á,** and for N sg. in **-é.**

M sg.	F sg.	N sg.
nový pokoj	**nová kuchyně**	**nové divadlo**
(new room)	(new kitchen)	(new theater)

Soft adjectives have one ending independent of gender: for M sg., F sg., and N sg. in **-í**

M sg.	F sg.	N sg.
moderní hotel	**moderní sukně**	**moderní auto**
(modern hotel)	(modern skirt)	(modern car)

Formation of adjectives with suffix **-cký, -ský**

M sg.	F sg.	N sg.
anglický čaj	**anglická škola**	**anglické jídlo**
(English tea)	(English school)	(English meal)

The comparative of adjectives ending with **-ý** is formed by removing the final **-ý** and adding **-ejší** or **-ší.** The superlative is formed by adding the prefix **nej-** to the comparative.

rychlý	**rychlejší**	**nejrychlejší**	fast-faster-fastest (regular)
dobrý	**lepší**	**nejlepší**	good-better-best (irregular)

The comparative and superlative of adjectives ending with **-í** have the same forms.

jižní	**jižnější**	**nejjižnější**	southern – more southern – most southern

POSSESSIVE ADJECTIVES

These adjectives express possession and are derived from nouns. They have hard endings.

sg M	F	N
otcův hotel	**otcova kniha**	**otcovo auto**
(father's hotel)	(father's book)	(father's car)
matčin hrad	**matčina láska**	**matčino město**
(mother's castle)	(mother's love)	(mother's town)

pl. Mi	F	N
otcovy hotely	**otcovy knihy**	**otcova auta**
(father's hotels)	(father's books)	(father's cars)

pl. Ma
otcovi přátelé
(father's friends)

Czech also has animate and inanimate forms for the masculine plural with different endings, e.g. **otcovi přátelé** (father's friends) is **Ma pl.**, with soft ending **-i**, and **otcovy hotely** (father's hotels) is **Mi pl.** with hard ending **-y**.

ADVERBS

In Czech there are two types of adverbs.

The first type (primary, not derived):

zde	here
brzy	soon
zítra	tomorrow

Stanice je zde.	The station is here.
Zítra jedeme.	We are departing tomorrow.

The second type (derived) is formed by removing the final **-ý** of the adjective and replacing it with **-e**, **-ě** or **-o**, **-y**.

pěkný	**pěkně**	nice - nicely
rychlý	**rychle**	quick - quickly

Venku je pěkně.   It is lovely outside.
Rychle zatoč doleva.   Turn around quickly to the left.

The comparative of adverbs is formed by adding **-eji** or **-ější**. For the superlative, add the prefix **nej-** to the comparative.

pěkně	**pěkněji**	**nejpěkněji**
nicely	more nicely	most nicely

SYNTAX

The Czech language has two basic sentence components – subject and predicate. This is the basic syntactical pair. For example:

Zemědelci pracují.   The farmers are working.

The noun masculine pl. animate **zemědelci** - farmers is the subject and v. 3.pl. **pracují** - (they) are working is the predicate.

Dívka spí.   The girl is sleeping.

The noun feminine sg. **dívka** - girl is the subject and v. 3.sg. **spí** - (she) is sleeping is the predicate.

| **Mám knihu.** | I have a book. (The personal pronoun "I" is not present in the Czech.) |

Here v. 1.sg. **mám** - (I) have is the predicate, **knihu** - book is the object, but the subject is missing. This is a *subjectless* sentence. Here are other examples:

Je teplo.	It is warm.
Je horko.	It is hot.
Je zima.	It is cold.
Prší.	It is raining.
Sněží.	It is snowing.
Mrzne.	It is freezing.
Je tam obsazeno?	Is that place (seat) taken?
Tady je volno.	The place is free.

Subject and Object

In English the difference between subject and object is expressed by the word order (the subject is followed by the object). In Czech the word order plays no role in expressing this. Here the cases come in. For example:

Eva má tu khihu.
Tu knihu má Eva.
Eva has this book.

Profesor má knihu.
The professor has a book.

In this sentence **professor** M sg. is the subject and **knihu** - book is the object. The predicate v. **mít** (to have) must be complemented by an object. It is a transitive verb.

In Czech the adjectives must agree with the nouns.
When the noun is M sg. or Ma pl., Mi pl., F sg. or
F pl. and N sg. or N pl., the adjective takes the same
gender (M, F, N) and number (sg. or pl.) of this
noun. For example:

M sg.	F sg.	N sg.
mladý můž	**heská žena**	**rostomilé zvíře**
young man	pretty woman	charming animal
Ma pl.	F pl.	N pl
mladí muži	**heské ženy**	**rostomolá zvířata**
young men	pretty women	charming animals
Mi pl.		
mladé stromy		
young trees		

To je velký pokoj.	This room is big.
Máte nový svetr.	You have a new sweater.

We can use two or more adjectives in a sentence.

Mám nový a heský svetr.
I have a new and nice sweater.

There are nouns which have the form of adjectives:

vrátný M sg., **vrátná** F sg. (porter).

Their declension follows the hard model of the
adjective **mladý** (young).

The verb also has to agree with the noun in the
sentence.

Mladí chlapci byli doma.
The young boys were at home. Ma pl.
Mladé stromy byly male.
The young trees were small. Mi pl.

Heské dívky byly doma.
The pretty girls were at home. F pl.
Auta jela rychle.
The cars were riding fast. N pl.

In third person plural there is a difference between
M, F, N: e.g. for Ma pl. the verb v. **být** (to be) takes
the soft ending **-i**; for Mi pl. and F pl. it takes the
hard ending **-y,** and for N pl. it takes the ending **-a**.
That is for *l-form* past tense.

CASES - PÁDY

The Czech language makes extensive use of cases –
forms taken by nouns, pronouns and adjectives to
show their relation to neighboring words in the sentence. There are seven cases (**pád** – case, abbreviation **p**.) in Czech. They have special rules, which
come mostly from the Old Slavonic (Old Bulgarian)
language of the ninth century A.D. Until today these
cases have kept almost the same function in the sentence and the same case endings in singular and
plural. We use specific "questions" to determine a
word's role in a sentence. The fifth case (vocative)
has no questions associated with it. Its name origi-
nates from Latin, meaning v. vocó, -áre – to call
(somebody), for example: **Páne!** Mister! Almost all
masculine, feminine and neuter nouns have declension according to the models given below.

CASES		Questions	Approximate English equivalent
1.nom.	nominative	**Kdo? Co?**	Who? What?
2.gen.	genitive	**Koho?**	Whose?
		Čeho?	Which?

3.dat.	dative	**Komu?**	Whom?
		Čemu?	Which?
4.acc.	accusative	**Koho?**	Whose?
		Co?	What?
5.voc.	vocative	no questions	
6.loc.	locative	**O kom?**	About whom?
		O čem?	About which?
7.instr.	instrumental	**S kým?**	With whom?
		S čím?	With what?

DECLENSION OF NOUNS

Masculine Nouns

Models

| **Hard** | **pán** (mister) animate |
| | **hrad** (castle) inanimate |

| **Soft** | **muž** (man) animate |
| | **stroj** (machine) inanimate |

| **Mixed** | **předseda** (chairman) hard animate |
| (hard and soft) | **soudce** (judge) soft animate |

sg.		pl.	
1p. pán	hrad	pani -ové	hrady
2p. pána	hradu	panů	hradů
3p. pánovi,-u	hradu	pánům	hradům
4p. pána	hrad	pány	hrady
5p. pane!	hrade!	páni!-ové!	hrady!
6p. (o) pánovi,-u	hradě	pánech	hradech
7p. (s) pánem	hradem	pány	hrady

sg.		pl.	
1p. muž	stroj	muži -ové	stroj
2p. muže	stroje	mužů	strojů
3p. mužovi, -i	stroje	mužům	strojům
4p. muže	stroj	muže	stroje
5p. muži!	stroji!	muži!-ové!	stroje!
6p. (o) mužovi,-i	stroji	mužích	strojích
7p. (s) mužem	strojem	muži	stroji

sg.		pl.	
1p. předseda	soudce	předsedové	soudci
2p. předsedy	soudce	předsedů	soudců
3p. předsedovi	soudci -ovi	předsedům	soudcům
4p. předsedu	soudce	předsedy	soudce
5p. předsedo!	soudce!	předsedové!	soudci!
6p. (o) předsedovi	soudci	předsedech	soudcích
7p. (s) předsedou	soudcem	předsedy	soudci

Feminine Nouns

Models

Hard žena (woman)

Soft nůše (back-basket)
   píseň (song)
   kost (bone)

sg.		pl.	
1p. žena	nůše	ženy	nůše
2p. ženy	nůše	žen	nůší
3p. ženě	nůši	ženám	nůším
4p. ženu	nůši	ženy	nůše
5p. ženo!	nůše!	ženy!	nůše!
6p. (o) ženě	nůši	ženách	nůších
7p. (s) ženou	nůší	ženami	nůšemi

sg.		pl.	
1p. píseň	kost	písně	kosti
2p. písně	kosti	písní	kostí
3p. písní	kosti	písním	kostem
4p. píseň	kost	písně	kosti
5p. písni!	kosti!	písně!	kosti!
6p. (o) písni	kosti	písních	kostech
7p. (s) písní	kostí	písněmi	kostmi

Neuter Nouns

Models

Hard **město** (town)

Soft **moře** (sea)

Mixed **kuře** (chicken)

Long **stavení** (building)

sg.		pl.	
1p. město	moře	města	moře
2p. města	moře	měst	moří
3p. městu	moři	městům	mořím
4p. město	moře	města	moře
5p. město!	moře!	města!	moře!
6p. (o) městě	moři	městech	mořích
7p. (s) městem	mořem	městy	moři

sg.		pl.	
1p. kuře	stavení	kuřata	stavení
2p. kuřete	stavení	kuřat	stavení
3p. kuřeti	stavení	kuřatům	stavením
4p. kuře	stavení	kuřata	stavení
5p. kuře!	stavení!	kuřata!	stavení!
6p. (o) kuřeti	stavení	kuřatech	staveních
7p. (s) kuřetem	stavením	kuřaty	staveními

DECLENSION OF ADJECTIVES

Models

Hard **mladý** (young)

Soft **jarní** (spring)

sg. M	F	N
1p. mladý muž	mladá žena	mladé kuře
2p. mladého	mládé	mladého
3p. mladému	mladé	mladému
4p. mladého	mladou	mladé
5p. mladý!	mladá!	mladé!
6p. (o) mladém	mladé	mladému
7p. (s) mladým	mladou	mladým

pl. 1p. mladé stromy (inanimate: young trees)

1p. mladí muži (animate)	mladé ženy	mladá kuřata
2p. mladých	mladých	mladých
3p. mladým	mladým	mladým
4p. mladé	mladé	mladá
5p. mladí!	mladé!	mladá!
6p. (o) mladých	mladých	mladých
7p. (s) mladým	mladými	mladými

sg. M	F	N	pl. M, F, N
1p. jarní	jarní	jarní	jarní
2p. jarního	jarní	jarního	jarních
3p. jarnímu	jarní	jarnímu	jarním
4p. jarního	jarní	jarní	jarní
5p. jarní!	jarní!	jarní!	jarní!
6p. (o) jarním	jarní	jarním	jarních
7p. (s) jarním	jarní	jarním	jarními

DECLENSION OF POSSESSIVE ADJECTIVES

Model

Hard   matčin (mother's)

sg.	M	F	N
1p.	matčin	matčina	matčino
2p.	matčina	matčiny	matčina
3p.	matčinu	matčině	matčinu
4p.	matčina	matčinu	matčino
5p.	matčin!	matčina!	matčino!
6p.	(o) matčině	matčině	matčině
	matčinu	matčinu	
7p.	(s) matčiným	matčinou	matčiným

pl.	M	F	N
1p.	matčini/y	matčiny	matčina
2p.	matčiných	matčiných	matčiných
3p.	matčiným	matčiným	matčiným
4p.	matčiny	matčiny	matčina
5p.	matčini/y!	matčiny!	matčina!
6p.	(o) matčiných	matčiných	matčiných
7p.	(s) matčinými	matčinými	matčinými

NOMINATIVE CASE

The nominative is the case of the subject in the sentence.

Obchod je otevřený. The **shop** is open.
Pavel přijel včera. **Pavel** arrived yesterday.
Ivana je učitelka. **Ivana** is a teacher.

GENITIVE CASE

The genitive is used to indicate that a noun depends on another noun. This case is often translated into English by means of *of*. It also is employed to express time by giving an answer to the question "when? At what time?", if a date is given.

mapa světa   map of **the world**
sklenice čaje   a cup of **tea**

Prepositions followed by the genitive.

od – do   from - to / till (time)
Pracujeme od rána do večera.
We work from dawn to dusk.

od   since
od té doby   since this time

až do   until
Spím až do rána.
I am sleeping until the morning.

do   within, by
Do týdně jsem zpátky.
I'll be back within a week.

Udělejte to do čtvrtka.
Make this by Thursday.

The days of the week.
do pondělka   until Monday

do   into
Dávám šaty do skříně.
I am putting my dress into the wardrobe.

z   from
Jsem z Prahy.
I am from Prague.

From a place to another place
z, ze ... do   from ... to
Jedu z Prahy do Brna.
I am traveling from Prague to Brno.

z, ze   of, out of
Sýr se dělá z mléka.
Cheese is made out of milk.

bez   without
dopis bez známky   letter without stamp

u   close to, at
Student stojí u stolu.
The student is standing close to the table.

vedle   beside, next to
Eva sedí vedle Marie.
Eva is sitting next to Mary.

místo   instead of
místo kamaráda   instead of a friend

během   during, in the course of
během večeře   during the dinner

podél   along
podél řeky   along the river

kolem = okolo   around, past, by, about
kolem stolu   around the table
kolem obchodního   by the mall
  domu
kolem druhé hodiny   about two o'clock

uprostřed		in the middle
uprostřed ulice		in the middle of the street
doprostřed		into the middle
doprostřed stolu		into the middle of the table
zprostřed		from the middle
zprostřed města		from the middle of the town
uvnitř		within, inside
uvnitř tašky je počítač		the computer is inside the bag
dovnitř		into
dovnitř klubovny (= do klubovny)		into the club
zevnitř		from within
zevnitř pokoje		from within the room
u		at
u nás		at our place

Partial genitive

The genitive also is used after weights and measures.

kilo	**kilo cukru**	one kilo of **sugar**
deko	**pět deka sýra**	50 grams of cheese
metr	**metr papíru**	one meter of paper
litr	**litr mléka**	one liter of milk
etc.		

Also after quantities.

kus	**kus chleba**	piece of bread
kousek	**kousek masa**	little piece of meat

půl	**půl litru mléka**	½ liter of milk
půlka	**půlka krabice**	half box of
čtvrt	**čtvrt hodiny**	quarter of an hour
čtvrtka	**čtvrtka chleba**	quarter of bread
talíř	**talíř polévky**	plate of soup
sklenice	**sklenice vody**	glass of water
láhev	**láhev vína**	bottle of wine
etc.		

DATIVE CASE

The dative is used for indirect objects with verbs like "to give" and "to send," depending on the direction of the activity. It implies giving (sending) something *to someone.*

Prepositions followed by the dative.

k, ke	to, towards
k němu	to **him**
proti	against
proti – naproti	opposite
naproti, /proti/	at the opposite side of
nám u stolu	the table
v, ve	in, at
pracuje v oboru fyziky	(S)he is working in the field of physics.
na	on, upon
na posteli	on the bed
na židli	on the chair
o	about
píše o ní	is written about her

po	after, along
po práci	after work
po dešti	after the rain
při	close by, near
při hradu	by the castle
vzhledem k	in view of considering
vůči	compared with
dík/y/	thanks
dík této práci	thanks to this work
kvůli	because of
kvůli tomu	because of this
vzdor, navzdory (=schválně=přes)	in spite of

ACCUSATIVE CASE

The object of most verbs is in the accusative case.

Chceme vidět starou Prahu.
We want to see **the old part of Prague**.

Prodáváte známky?
Do you sell **stamps**?

Mohu použít Váš telefon?
May I use **your phone**?

Objects:
starou Prahu	the old part of Prague
známky	stamps
Váš telefon	your phone

Prepositions followed by the accusative.

na   onto, to
Jedeme na hory.
We are going to the mountains.

přes   across, through
přes ulici   across the street
Půjdu přes park.   I'll pass through
                                     the park.

VOCATIVE CASE

The vocative case is used when one is addressing
somebody.

Pane doktore!   Doctor!
Dámy a pánové!   Ladies and gentlemen!

LOCATIVE CASE

This case is used with prepositions and usually indicates location and direction.

na   on
na stole   on **the table**
na ulici   in **the street**

o   about
o kočkách   about cats

v, ve   in, on
v Praze   in Prague
v sobotu   on Saturday

po	after
po večeři	after dinner
po Vás	after you

INSTRUMENTAL CASE

The instrumental case is used to show by whom or how an action is performed.

Jedu vlakem.
I am traveling by **train**.

It is used with prepositions to express place.

před	in front of, before
před domem	in front of **the home**
před Vánocemi	before **Christmas**

za	behind, beyond
za divadlem	behind the theater
za rohem	behind the corner
za jezerem	beyond the lake
mezi	between, among
mezi sebou	between us
mezi lidmi	among people

nad	over, above
nad stolem	above the desk
nad nulou	above zero

pod	under, below
pod nulou	below zero
pod mostem	under the bridge

To express time

před	(to express before)
před týdnem	**a week** ago
před rokem	**a year** ago
před hodinou	**one hour** ago
s/e/	together, with
se mnou	with me
s Pavlem	with Paul
s rodiči	with the parents

CZECH-ENGLISH DICTIONARY

Note: slashes (//) are used to denote verbal aspect prefixes. For example, /po/zvednout (raise) indicates that "po" is added to make the perfective form of the verb.

A

a *conj.* and
abeceda *n.* alphabet
ačkoli *conj.* although
adoptovat *v.* adopt
adresa *n.* address
advokát *n.* lawyer
agentura *n.* agency
ahoj *interj.* bye
ahoj *interj.* hello
akademický *adj.* academic
aktivita *n.* activity
aktivní *adj.* active
ale *conj.* but
alternativní *adj.* alternative
americký *adj.* American
Američan *n.* American
analýza *n.* analysis
analyzovat *v.* analyze
ananas *n.* pineapple
anglický *adj.* English
ano *adv.* yes
apelovat (na) *v.* appeal
armáda *n.* army
asi *adv.* about

auto *n.* car
autobus *n.* bus
autor *n.* author
až *prep.* until

B

báječný *adj.* wonderful
bajka *n.* fable
bakterie *n.* bacteria
balíček *n.* packet
balík *n.* package
balit *v.* pack
balkón *n.* balcony
banální *adj.* banal
banán *n.* banana
banka *n.* bank
bankovka *n.* bill
bankovnictví *n.* banking
barokní *adj.* baroque
barva *n.* color; paint
bát se *v.* afraid
bavlna *n.* cotton
bazén *n.* swimming pool
běh *n.* run; race
během *prep.* during
beletrie *n.* fiction
benzín *n.* gasoline
bez *prep.* without
bezpečnost *n.* security
bezpečný *adj.* safe
bílý *adj.* white
blahopřát *v.* congratulate
blízký *adj.* close
bolest *n.* pain
bonbón *n.* candy

bota *n.* shoe
brada *n.* beard; chin
brambor *n.* potato
brána *n.* gate
bránit *v.* defend
branka *n.* goal
bratr *n.* brother
broskev *n.* peach
brzy *adv.* soon
březen *n.* March
budoucí *adj.* future
budoucnonost *n.* future
burský oříšek *n.* peanut
bydlet *v.* live
byt *n.* apartment
být *v.* be
být v čele *v.* head

C

celer *n.* celery
celkový *adj.* total
celý *adj.* whole; entire
cement *n.* cement
cena *n.* award; cost; price; prize
cent *n.* cent
centrální *adj.* central
centrum města *n.* downtown
cesta *n.* journey; tour; trip; drive; route; way
cestička *n.* path
cestování *n.* travel
cestovat *v.* travel
cestující *n.* passenger
cibule *n.* onion
cigareta *n.* cigarette
cihla *n.* brick

cíl *n.* aim
cit *n.* feeling
citoslovce *n. pl. gram.* interjection
citovat *v.* quote
citrón *n.* lemon
cizí *adj.* foreign
co *pron.* what
cukr *n.* sugar
cukroví *n.* confectionery

Č

čaj *n.* tea
čára *n.* line
čas *n.* time
čas (u doktora) *n.* (to make an) appointment
časopis *n.* magazine
část *n.* part
částečně *adv.* partly
částíce *n. gram.* particle
částka *n.* amount
často *adv.* often
Čechy *n.* Bohemia
čekat *v.* await; wait
čelo *n.* forehead
čepice *n.* cap
černý *adj.* black
čerstvý *adj.* fresh
červen *n.* June
červenec *n.* July
červený *adj.* red
český *adj.* Czech; Bohemian
čin *n.* act
činnost *n.* action
čirý *adj.* clear

číslo *n.* number; figure
číslovka *n. gram.* number
číst *v.* read
čistý *adj.* clean
číšník *n.* waiter
článek *n.* link
člen *n.* member
členství *n.* membership
člověk *n.* person
čokoláda *n.* chocolate
čtvrt *n.* quarter
čtvrtek *n.* Thursday
čtyři *num.* four

D

dál *adv.* on
dále *adv.* farther
daleko *adv.* far
dalekohled *n.* binoculars
daleký *adj.* faraway
další *adj.* other; another; further
dar *n.* gift
dárek *n.* present
darovat *v.* donate
dát *v.* give; put; place
datum *n.* date
dávat přednost *v.* prefer
dbát *v.* mind
debata *n.* debate
dech *n.* breath
deka *n.* blanket
děkovat *v.* thank
dělat *v.* do; make
dělit se *v.* divide

délka *n.* length
den *n.* day (pl. dni)
deník *n.* diary
denní *adj.* daily
deset *num.* ten
deska *n.* board
déšť *n.* rain
deštník *n.* umbrella
detail *n.* detail
děťátko *n.* baby
devět *num.* nine
dieta *n.* diet
dík *n.* thanks
díl *n.* share
díra *n.* gap; hole
disketa *n.* diskette
diskuse *n.* debate
diskutovat *v.* argue
dítě *n.* child; kid (pl. děti)
divadlo *n.* theater
dívat se *v.* look; watch
dívka *n.* girl
dlouhý *adj.* long
dnes *adv.* today
do *prep.* into
doba *n.* term
dobro *n.* good
dobrý *adj.* good
dobře *adv.* well
dodat *v.* add
dodatek *n.* addition
dohoda *n.* deal
dohromady *adv.* together
dojem *n.* impression
dokázat *v.* prove
dokonalý *adj.* perfect

doleva *adv.* left
dolů *adv.* down; below
domácí *adj.* domestic
domácnost *n.* household
dopadnout *v.* capture
dopis *n.* letter
doplňkový *adj.* additional
dopoledne *n.* A.M.
doporučit *v.* recommend
doprava *n.* traffic; transport
doprovodit *v.* accompany
dopředu *adv.* forward
dosáhnout *v.* achieve
dospělý *adj.* adult
dost *adv.* enough; quite
dostat *v.* get, receive
dosud *adv.* still
dotaz *n.* inquiry
dotek *n.* touch
dotknout se *v.* touch
doufat *v.* hope
doutník *n.* cigar
dovnitř *adv.* in
dovolená *n.* vacation
dovolit *v.* allow; let; permit
dovolit si *v.* afford
drahý *adj.* dear; beloved; expensive; costly
drůbež *n.* poultry
druh *n.* kind; sort
druhý *adj.* second
držet *v.* hold
dřevěné uhlí *n.* charcoal
dřivější *adj.* former; prior
duben *n.* April
důkaz *n.* evidence
důležitost *n.* importance

důležitý *adj.* important
dům *n.* home; house (pl. domy)
důstojnost *n.* dignity
důvěra *n.* faith
důvěřovat *v.* trust
důvod *n.* reason; argument
dva *num.* two
dvakrát *num.* twice
dveře *n.* door
dvojitý *adj.* double
dvůr *n.* yard
džem *n.* jam

E

elegantní *adj.* elegant
elektronická pošta *n.* e-mail
elektronika *n.* electronics
elektřina *n.* electricity
elementární *adj.* basic
energie *n.* energy

F

fajn *interj.* okay
fanda *n.* fan
fazole *n.* bean
film *n.* film
finance *n.* finance
fond *n.* fund
formulace *n.* statement
fotbal *n.* soccer
fotoaparát *n.* camera
fotografie *n.* photograph
funkce *n.* function

G

garáž *n.* garage
generace *n.* generation
generál *n.* general
gotický *adj.* Gothic
gramatický *adj.* grammatical
grilovat *v.* grill
guláš *n.* goulash

H

hádka *n.* quarrel
halenka *n.* blouse
hezký *adj.* pretty
historický *adj.* historic
historie *n.* history
hlad *n.* hunger; famine
hlas *n.* voice
hlasování *n.* vote
hlava *n.* head
hlavní *adj.* main
hlavní město *n.* capital
hledat *v.* search; seek
hlídka *n.* guard
hloubka *n.* depth
hluboce *adv.* deeply
hluboký *adj.* deep
hluk *n.* noise
hmat *n.* feeling
hmyz *n.* insect
hnědý *adj.* brown
hodina *n.* hour
hodinky *n. pl.* watch
hodiny *n. pl.* clock

hodit *v.* throw
hodnota *n.* value
hojit se *v.* heal
holič *n.* barber
hora *n.* mountain
horečka *n.* fever
horký *adj.* hot
horní *adj.* upper
hořký *adj.* bitter
hospoda *n.* pub
hostina *n.* feast
hotel *n.* hotel
houba *n.* mushroom
hovězí maso *n.* beef
hovořit *v.* converse
hra *n.* game; play
hračka *n.* toy
hrad *n.* castle
hranice *n.* limit
hrát *v.* play
hrdý *adj.* proud
hrozinka *n.* raisin
hroznové zrnko *n.* grape
hřeben *n.* comb
hudba *n.* music
hvězda *n.* star

CH

chlad *n.* cold; chill
chladný *adj.* cool
chlapec *n.* boy
chléb *n.* bread
chodba *n.* corridor
chránit *v.* protect
chtít *v.* want; intend
chuť *n.* taste

chvála *n.* praise
chvástat se *v.* brag
chvíle *n.* while
chyba *n.* mistake
chytat *v.* catch
chytrý *adj.* clever

I

i *conj.* and; also
identita *n.* identity
ilustrovat *v.* illustrate
inflace *n.* inflation
informace *n.* information
informovat *v.* inform
iniciativa *n.* initiative
inkoust *n.* ink
investice *n.* investment

J

já *pron.* I
jablko *n.* apple
jaderný *adj.* nuclear
jak *adv.* how
jako *adv.* as; like
jaro *n.* spring
játra *n.* liver
jazyk *n.* language; speech; tongue
jeden *adj.* single
jeden *num.* one
jeden *pron.* either
jednat *v.* discuss
jednatelství *n.* agency
jednoduchý *adj.* simple
jednotlivec *n.* individual

jednotné číslo *n. gram.* singular
jednou *adv.* once .
jehla *n.* needle
jehně *n.* lamb
jeho *pron.* his
jeskyně *n.* cave
jestliže *conj.* if
ji *pron.* her
jich *pron.* them
jídlo *n.* food; meal
jih *n.* south
jim *pron.* them
jinak *adv.* otherwise
jiný *adj.* else
jiný *pron.* other
jíst *v.* eat
jistý *adj.* certain; sure
jít *v.* go; walk
jízda *n.* drive
jméno *n.* name
jmenovat *v.* appoint

K

k *prep.* towards; by
kabát *n.* coat
kabelka *n.* handbag
kakao *n.* cocoa
kalendář *n.* calendar
kalhoty *n. pl.* pants
kam *adv.* where
kancelář *n.* office; agency
kantýna *n.* cafeteria
kapesník *n.* handkerchief
kapitán *n.* captain
kapitola *n.* chapter

kapka *n.* drop
kapsa *n.* pocket
karafiát *n.* carnation
kari *n.* curry
kartáček na zuby *n.* toothbrush
kartón *n.* card
kašel *n.* cough
katolický *adj.* Catholic
káva *n.* coffee
kavalír *n.* gentleman
kavárna *n.* café
kaviár *n.* caviar
kázat *v.* preach
každodenní *adj.* everyday
každý *adj.* each; every
kbelík *n.* bucket
kde *adv.* where
kdekoli *adv.* anywhere
kdo *pron.* who
kdy *adv.* when
když *conj.* as
keks *n.* biscuit
kino *n.* cinema
klečet *v.* kneel
klíč *n.* key
klinika *n.* clinic
klobouk *n.* hat
kloub *n.* joint
kluk *n.* guy
knedlík *n.* dumpling
kniha *n.* book
knihař *n.* binder
knihovna *n.* library; bookcase
knoflík *n.* button
kočka *n.* cat
kokos *n.* coconut
koláč *n.* cake

kolega *n.* partner
kolej *n.* dormitory
kolem *adv.* around
koleno *n.* knee
kolik *pron.* what
kolo *n.* bicycle
komín *n.* chimney
komnata *n.* chamber
koncert *n.* concert
konec *n.* end; finish
konečně *adv.* finally
konečný *adj.* final
konečný termín *n.* deadline
konstrukce *n.* frame
konto *n.* account
kontrola *n.* check
konvice *n.* kettle
kopec *n.* hill
kopie *n.* copy
kopnutí *n.* kick
kořen *n.* root
koření *n.* spice
kostel *n.* church
košíková *n.* basketball
kotleta *n.* cutlet
koupat se *v.* bathe
koupel *n.* bath
koupelna *n.* bathroom
koupit *v.* buy
kouřit *v.* smoke
kousek *n.* bit; cut
krabice *n.* box; carton
král *n.* king
králík *n.* rabbit
královna *n.* queen
královský *adj.* royal

krásný *adj.* beautiful
krátký *adj.* short
kredit *n.* credit
kreslení *n.* drawing
kreslit *v.* draw
krev *n.* blood
kriket *n.* cricket
kritický *adj.* critical
krk *n.* neck; throat
krmení *n.* feed
krok *n.* step
kroket *n.* croquet
kromě *prep.* except
kromě toho *adv.* besides
kruh *n.* circle
krutý *adj.* cruel
krvácet *v.* bleed
krystal *n.* crystal
křída *n.* chalk
křik *n.* cry
který *pron.* which
kuchyně *n.* kitchen
kufr *n.* suitcase
kukuřice *n.* corn
kulečník *n.* billiards
kulturní *adj.* cultural
kůň *n.* horse
kuře *n.* chicken
kus *n.* piece
kvalita *n.* quality
květ *n.* bloom
květák *n.* cauliflower
květen *n.* May
květina *n.* flower
kyselina *n.* acid
kytice *n.* bouquet

L

láhev *n.* bottle
lampa *n.* lamp
láska *n.* love
látka *n.* material
lavička *n.* bench
léčba *n.* treatment; cure
led *n.* ice
leden *n.* January
lednička *n.* refrigerator
ledvina *n.* kidney
legrační *adj.* funny
lehký *adj.* easy
lék *n.* drug
lékárna *n.* drugstore; pharmacy
lékař *n.* physician; doctor
lékařský *adj.* medical
lekce *n.* lesson
lepidlo *n.* glue
les *n.* forest; wood
let *n.* flight
letadlo *n.* airplane; plane
létat *v.* fly
letiště *n.* airport
léto *n.* summer
lev *n.* lion
levný *adj.* cheap
ležák *n.* lager
ležet *v.* lie
lidé *n.* folk
lidský *adj.* human
límec *n.* collar
list *n.* leaf
lístek *n.* ticket
listopad *n.* November
loď *n.* ship

loďka *n.* boat
ložnice *n.* bedroom
ložní prádlo *n. pl.* bedclothes
lupy *n.* dandruff
lžíce *n.* spoon

M

majitel *n.* owner
malba *n.* painting
málo *adv.* little; few
malovat *v.* paint
malý *adj.* small
manipulovat *v.* manipulate
manžel *n.* husband
manželka *n.* wife
manželství *n.* marriage
mapa *n.* map
máslo *n.* butter
maso *n.* meat; flesh
mastný *adj.* greasy
matka *n.* mother
mě *pron.* me
med *n.* honey
mechanik *n.* mechanic
měkký *adj.* soft
méně *adv.* less
menšina *n.* minority
meruňka *n.* apricot
měřítko *n.* scale
měsíc *n.* month
město *n.* city; town
městský *adj.* urban
metoda *n.* method
metro *n.* subway
mezi *prep.* among; between

mezinárodní *adj.* international
mezitím *adv.* meanwhile
mi *pron.* me
míč *n.* ball
miláček *n.* darling
milovat *v.* love
mimořádný *adj.* extraordinary
mince *n.* coin
minulost *n.* past
minulý *adj.* past
minuta *n.* minute
mír *n.* peace
míra *n.* measure
mísa *n.* dish
místní *adj.* local
místní občan *n.* resident
místo *n.* place; position; space
místo *prep.* instead
mít *v.* have
mít rád *v.* like
mít úspěch *v.* succeed
mládí *n.* youth
mladý *adj.* young
mlékárna *n.* dairy
mléko *n.* milk
mlha *n.* fog
mluvit *v.* talk
mne *pron.* me
mně *pron.* me
mnohdy *adv.* frequently
mnoho *adj.* many
mnoho *adv.* much
množné číslo *n. gram.* plural
množství *n.* quantity
moci *v.* can; may
moč *n.* urine
móda *n.* fashion; trend

moderní *adj.* modern
módní výstřelek *n.* fad
modrý *adj.* blue
mohl bych *v.* might
mokrý *adj.* wet
moře *n.* sea
most *n.* bridge
motor *n.* motor
motýl *n.* butterfly
moučník *n.* dessert
mouka *n.* flour
možná *adv.* perhaps; maybe
možnost *n.* chance; option; possibility; opinion
možný *adj.* potential
mrak *n.* cloud
mrkev *n.* carrot
mrknutí *n.* blink
muset *v.* must
muzeum *n.* museum
muž *n.* man
mužský *adj.* male
my *pron.* we
mýdlo *n.* soap
mysl *n.* mind
myslet *v.* think
myšlenka *n.* idea; thought
mzda *n.* wage

N

na *prep.* at; in; on
nabídka *n.* offer
nabídnout *v.* offer
náboženstí *n.* religion
nad *prep.* over
nadaný *adj.* talented

naděje *n.* hope
nahlas *adv.* aloud
nahoře *adv.* up; above
nájemné *n.* rent
najít *v.* find
najmout *v.* engage
nakupování *n.* shopping
nalehavý *adj.* urgent
nalodit se *v.* embark
náměstí *n.* square
naneštěstí *adv.* unfortunately
napadnout *v.* attack
na palubě *adv.* aboard
naplnit *v.* fill
napodobovat *v.* imitate
nápoj *n.* drink; beverage
napravo *adv.* right
naprosto *adv.* absolutely
naproti *prep.* against
napřed *adv.* ahead
náramek *n.* bangle; bracelet
náraz *n.* impact
národní *adj.* national
narozen *adj.* born
narození *n.* birth
narozeniny *n. pl.* birthday
nařídit *v.* order
následovat *v.* follow
následující *adj.* following
nástroj *n.* instrument
náušnice *n.* earring
navíc *adj.* extra
návrat *n.* return
návrh *n.* proposal
návrhář *n.* designer
návštěva *n.* visit
návštěvník *n.* guest

navštívit *v.* visit
navždy *adv.* forever
na zdraví *interj.* cheers
naznačit *v.* imply
nazvat *v.* name
ne *part.* no; not
nebezpečí *n.* danger
nebo *conj.* or
něco *pron.* anything
nedaleký *adj.* nearby
nedávno *adv.* recently
neděle *n.* Sunday
nedostatek *n.* lack; defect
nehet *n.* nail
nehoda *n.* accident
nějaký *adj.* any; some
nejlepší *adj.* best
nejmenší *adj.* smallest
nejvíc *adv.* most
někdo *pron.* anybody
několik *num.* several
nemocnice *n.* hospital
nemocný *adj.* ill
nemocný *n.* sick person; patient
nemožný *adj.* impossible
nenávidět *v.* hate
nepřítomnost *n.* absence
neschopný *adj.* unable
nesouhlasit *v.* disagree
nesprávný *adj.* wrong
nést *v.* carry
nezaměstnanost *n.* unemployment
nezávislost *n.* independence
nezávislý *adj.* independent
nezbytný *adj.* vital
neznámý *adj.* unknown
nezvyklý *adj.* unusual

nic *pron.* nothing
nicméně *adv.* nevertheless
nikdo *pron.* nobody; none
nikdy *adv.* never
nit *n.* thread
nízký *adj.* low
níže *adv.* below
noc *n.* night
noha *n.* foot; leg
nos *n.* nose
nosit *v.* carry; wear
noviny *n.* newspaper
nový *adj.* new
nula *n.* zero
nutnost *n.* need
nutný *adj.* necessary
nůž *n.* knife
nůžky *n. pl.* scissors

O

obálka *n.* envelope; wrapper
občan *n.* citizen
občerstvení *n.* refreshment
obdivovat se *v.* admire
období *n.* period
obdržet *v.* obtain
obecně *adv.* generally
oběd *n.* lunch
obědvat *v.* have lunch
obehnat *v.* enclose
obezřetelný *adj.* cautious
obchod *n.* shop; store; trade
obchodní dohoda *n.* bargain
obilovina *n.* cereal
objednat se *v.* make an appointment (with the doctor)

objevit *v.* discover
oblast *n.* region
oblečení *n.* clothes
oblek *n.* suit
obličej *n.* face
obloha *n.* sky
obratel *n.* vertebra
obrátit se *v.* appeal
obraz *n.* picture; image
obřad *n.* ceremony
obsahovat *v.* contain
obviňování *n.* blame
obvyklý *adj.* usual; normal
obyčejný *adj.* ordinary
obžalovat *v.* accuse
ocenit *v.* evaluate
oceňovat *v.* appreciate
ocet *n.* vinegar
očekávat *v.* expect
očkování *n.* vaccination
oční kapky *n. pl.* eyedrops
odborník *n.* expert
odděleně *adv.* separately
oddělený *adj.* separate
odemknout *v.* unlock
odchod *n.* departure
odjet *v.* depart
odmítnout *v.* refuse; reject
odpadky *n.* garbage
odpočinek *n.* rest
odpoledne *n.* afternoon; P.M.
odpor *n.* dislike
odpovědět *v.* answer; reply
odpověď *n.* response; answer
odpovídat *v.* respond; account
odpustit *v.* forgive

odvolat *v.* cancel
oficiální *adj.* formal
oheň *n.* fire
ohlásit *v.* announce
ohodnotit *v.* assess
ohrada *n.* fence
ohromný *adj.* huge; vast
ohyb *n.* bend
ochrana *n.* protection
ochutnat *v.* taste
okamžitě *adv.* immediately
okamžitý *adj.* immediate
okno *n.* window
oko *n.* eye
okolo *adv.* around
okraj *n.* edge
okurka *n.* cucumber
olej *n.* oil
omáčka *n.* sauce; gravy
on *pron.* he
ona *pron.* she
oni, ony *pron.* they
opakovat *v.* repeat
opatrný *adj.* cautious; wary
opatřit *v.* provide
opět *adv.* again; anew
opilý *adj.* drunk
opozice *n.* opposition
oprava *n.* repair
opravdu *adv.* actually
opustit *v.* leave; abandon
oranžový *adj.* orange
organizace *n.* organization; association
organizovat *v.* organize; plan
ořech *n.* nut
osm *num.* eight
/o/smažit *v.* fry

ostrov *n.* island
osvědčení *n.* certificate
ošetřovat *v.* treat
ošklivý *adj.* ugly
otázka *n.* question
otec *n.* father
otevřeně *adv.* baldly
otevření *n.* opening
otevřený *adj.* open
otevřít *v.* open; begin
otočení *n.* turn
otočit *v.* turn
ovesná kaše *n.* porridge
ovládat *v.* command
ovlivnit *v.* influence
ovoce *n.* fruit
ovzduší *n.* atmosphere
označit *v.* mark; indicate; designate
oznámení *n.* notice
oznámit *v.* announce
oženit se *v.* marry

P

pád *n.* fall
padnout *v.* fit
pak *adv.* after; then
palačinka *n.* pancake
pán *n.* Mr.; sir; lord
panenka *n.* doll
pánev *n.* pan
paní *n.* madam; Mrs.; lady
papír *n.* paper
pár *n.* pair
pardon *interj.* sorry
park *n.* park

parkoviště *n.* parking
parlament *n.* parliament
pas *n.* passport; waist
páska *n.* tape
pasta na zuby *n.* toothpaste
pátek *n.* Friday
páteř *n.* backbone
patřičný *adj.* appropriate
patřit *v.* belong
pažitka *n.* chives
péci *v.* bake
péče *n.* care
pečení *n.* baking
pečovat *v.* care
pekárna *n.* bakery
pekař *n.* baker
pěkný *adj.* nice; fine
pěna *n.* foam
peněženka *n.* wallet
peníze *n.* money; cash
pero *n.* pen
pes *n.* dog
pěstovat *v.* grow
pět *num.* five
pevnit *v.* fix
pevný *adj.* strong; firm
piknik *n.* barbecue
pilně *adv.* hard
píseň *n.* song
písmo *n.* writing
pít *v.* drink
pití *n.* drinking
pivo *n.* beer
placení *n.* payment
pláč *n.* cry
plán *n.* project; plan
plat *n.* pay

plavat *v.* swim
pláž *n.* beach
plenka *n.* diaper
plést *v.* knit
pleť *n.* skin
plíce *n. pl.* lungs
plně *adv.* fully
plný *adj.* full
plocha *n.* area
plot *n.* fence
plyn *n.* gas
pneumatika *n.* tire
po *prep.* throughout; along
pocit *n.* feel
poctít *v.* dignify
počasí *n.* weather
počáteční *adj.* initial
počítač *n.* computer
pod *prep.* under
podívat se *v.* glance
podlaha *n.* floor
podle *prep.* according
podnik *n.* firm
podobně *adv.* similarly
podobný *adj.* alike
podstatné jméno *n. gram.* noun
podzim *n.* autumn; fall
pohled *n.* look
pohlednice *n.* postcard
pohovor *n.* interview
pohyb *n.* move
pojištění *n.* insurance
pokladna *n.* ticket office
pokladník *n.* cashier
poklice *n.* cover
pokoj *n.* room; bedroom
pokračovat *v.* continue

pokrok *n.* progress
pokřikovat *v.* shout
pokus *n.* attempt
pole *n.* field
poledne *n.* midday; noon
polemika *n.* dispute
polévka *n.* soup
polibek *n.* kiss
policie *n.* police
policista *n.* policeman
položit *v.* lay
polštář *n.* pillow
pomalý *adj.* slow
pomeranč *n.* orange
pomlouvat *v.* backbite
pomoc *n.* aid; help; assistance
pomoci *v.* help
pondělí *n.* Monday
/po/nechat *v.* keep
poněkud *adv.* rather
popel *n.* ash
poplatek *n.* tax
popřít *v.* deny
poradit *v.* advise
porážka *n.* defeat
porcelán *n.* china
pořadí *n.* order
poskytnout *v.* grant
poslat *v.* send
poslední *adj.* last
poslouchat *v.* listen; obey
posluchači *n.* audience
postavit *v.* build
postel *n.* bed
postup *n.* advance; proceeding
poškození *n.* damage
pošta *n.* post; mail

potěšený *adj.* glad
potkat *v.* meet
potleskat *v.* clap
potom *adv.* after; afterwards
potraviny *n. pl.* groceries, provisions
potřebovat *v.* need
potvrdit *v.* certify
potvrzený *adj.* confirmed
pouze *adv.* only
považovat *v.* regard
pověřovat *v.* impose
pověsit *v.* hang
povinnost *n.* duty; obligation
povolání *n.* profession
povolení *n.* permit
povolit *v.* allow
povýšit *v.* promote
povzbuzovat *v.* encourage
pozdější *adj.* latter
pozdní *adj.* late
pozdrav *n.* greeting
poznamenat *v.* note
poznámka *n.* note; reference
poznat *v.* identify; recognize
pozornost *n.* attention
pozorování *n.* observation
pozorovat *v.* observe
poznání *n.* cognition
pozvat *v.* invite
/po/zvednout *v.* raise
požádat *v.* apply
požadavek *n.* demand
práce *n.* work; job; labor
pracovat *v.* work
pracovník *n.* worker
pračka *n.* washing machine
prach *n.* dust

prášek *n.* powder
prát *v.* wash
pravda *n.* truth
pravděpodobný *adv.* probably
pravdivý *adj.* true
právě *adv.* just
pravidelný *adj.* regular
pravidlo *n.* rule
pravomoc *n.* authority
prázdný *adj.* empty
pro *prep.* for
problém *n.* trouble
proč *adv.* why
prodávat *v.* sell
prodej *n.* sale
program *n.* agenda
prohlížet si *v.* view
prohra *n.* defeat
projít *v.* pass
promenáda *n.* esplanade
pronásledovat *v.* pursue
prosinec *n.* December
proslulý *adj.* famous
prosím *interj.* please
proti *prep.* against
protože *conj.* because
proud *n.* flow
provést *v.* perform
prsa *n.* breast
prst *n.* finger
prst na noze *n.* toe
prsten *n.* ring
průchod *n.* passage
průjem *n.* diarrhea
průmysl *n.* industry
průmyslový *adj.* industrial

průvodce *n.* guide
pružný *adj.* elastic
první *adj.* first; prime
pryč *adv.* away; off
přátelský *adj.* friendly
přátelství *n.* fellowship; friendship
přát si *v.* wish
před *adv.* ago
před *prep.* before
předek *n.* front
předložka *n. gram.* preposition
předmět *n.* object; item; subject
předmluva *n.* preface
přední *adj.* front
přednost *n.* priority
předpoklad *n.* assumption
předpokládat *v.* suppose; assume
předsíň *n.* hall
představení *n.* performance
představit *v.* introduce
představit si *v.* imagine
předtím *adv.* previously
předvést *v.* present
přehrada *n.* dam
překvapení *n.* surprise
přerušit *v.* interrupt
přes *prep.* through; across; via
přesčas *n.* overtime
přestat *v.* cease
přestěhovat se *v.* move
přesunout *v.* shift
příběh *n.* story
přiblížení *n.* approach
příčina *n.* cause
přidání *n.* addition
přidat *v.* add
přídavné jméno *n. gram.* adjective

příchod *n.* approach; arrival
příjem *n.* income
příjezd *n.* entry
přijít *v.* come; arrive
přijmout *v.* accept
přikázat *v.* command
příklad *n.* example; case; instance
přileřitost *n.* opportunity
přímení *n.* surname
přímý *adj.* direct
přinést *v.* bring
přínos *n.* asset
přinutit *v.* force
připevnit *v.* attach
příprava *n.* preparation
připravený *adj.* ready
připravit *v.* prepare
připustit *v.* admit
příroda *n.* nature
přírodní *adj.* natural
příslovce *n. gram.* adverb
přistát *v.* land
přístav *n.* port
příští *adj.* next
přístup *n.* access
přístupný *adj.* available
přitažlivý *adj.* attractive
přítel *n.* friend
přítomný *adj.* present
přiznat *v.* acknowledge
psací stůl *n.* desk
psát *v.* write
pták *n.* bird
ptát se *v.* ask; question
půda *n.* soil
půjčka *n.* loan

půlka *n.* half
působit *v.* affect
půvab *n.* charm
původní *adj.* original
pytel *n.* sack

R

rada *n.* advice
radost *n.* pleasure; joy
rajče *n.* tomato
rameno *n.* shoulder
rána *n.* wound
ráno *n.* morning
recepce *n.* banquet
recept *n.* prescription
rejstřík *n.* index
rektor *n.* principal
rentgenový paprsek *n.* X-ray
republika *n.* republic
restaurace *n.* restaurant
ret *n.* lip
revoluce *n.* revolution
roční *adj.* annual
roční doba *n.* season
rodič *n.* parent
rodina *n.* family
rok *n.* year
rolník *n.* farmer
rosa *n.* dew
rostlina *n.* plant
rovněž *adv.* also
rovnou *adv.* baldly; directly
rovný *adj.* even; flat; level
rozbít *v.* break
rozbor *n.* analysis

rozdíl *n.* difference
rozehnat *v.* disperse
rozhněvaný *adj.* angry
rozhovor *n.* talk
rozkošný *adj.* lovely
rozloučení *n.* farewell
rozpustit se *v.* dissolve
rozsvítit *v.* light
roztomilý *adj.* cute
roztrhnutí *n.* tear
rozumět *v.* understand
rozumný *adj.* reasonable
rozvinout *v.* develop
rozvod *n.* divorce
ručník *n.* towel
ruka *n.* hand; arm
rukavice *n.* glove
růst *n.* growth
rušit *v.* disturb
růžový *adj.* pink
rvačka *n.* fight
rvát se *v.* fight
ryba *n.* fish
rychle *adv.* quickly; rapidly
rychlý *adj.* quick; fast
ryže *n.* rice

Ř

řada *n.* series
ředitel *n.* manager; director
řeka *n.* river
řetěz *n.* chain
říci *v.* speak; tell; say
řidič *n.* driver; chauffeur
řídit *v.* lead

řídký *adj.* rare
říjen *n.* October
říznout se *v.* cut
říznutí *n.* cut

S

s *prep.* with
sahat *v.* reach
sako *n.* jacket
sám *adj.* alone
samice *n.* female
samoobsluha *n.* supermarket
sanitka *n.* ambulance
sbírat *v.* collect
scéna *n.* scene
sdružovat *v.* associate
sedět *v.* sit
sedm *num.* seven
sekretář *n.* secretary
selhat *v.* fail
sen *n.* dream
sepsat *v.* list
/se/ rozhodnout *v.* decide
sestra *n.* sister; nurse
sestup *n.* descent
sestupovat *v.* descend
sever *n.* north
/se/ vzbudit *v.* wake up
seznam *n.* list
shromáždění *n.* assembly
shromáždit *v.* gather
schopný *adj.* able
schůze *n.* meeting
schůzka *n.* appointment
schvalovat *v.* approve

síla *n.* power; force
silnice *n.* road
silný *adj.* thick
sirup *n.* syrup
síť *n.* network
sjednotit *v.* unite
sklo *n.* glass
skoro *adv.* almost
skořice *n.* cinnamon
skupina *n.* group
skutečnost *n.* fact
skutečný *adj.* real; actual
skvrna *n.* spot
skákat *v.* jump
slabý *adj.* faint; weak
sladký *adj.* sweet
slanina *n.* bacon
sláva *n.* fame
slavit *v.* celebrate
slavnost *n.* ceremony
slavnostní *adj.* festive
slečna *n.* Miss
sleva *n.* discount
slíbit *v.* promise
sloveso *n. gram.* verb
slovník *n.* dictionary
slovo *n.* word
sluha *n.* servant
slunce *n.* sun
slunit se *v.* bask
služba *n.* service
služebná *n.* maid
slyšet *v.* hear
slza *n.* tear
smát se *v.* laugh
směrem *prep.* onto
smetana *n.* cream

smíchat *v.* mix
snaha *n.* aspiration
snídaně *n.* breakfast
snížení *n.* decrease
sobota *n.* Saturday
sotva *adv.* hardly
soudce *n.* judge
soudit *v.* judge
souhlas *n.* agreement; assent
souhlasit *v.* agree
soukromý *adj.* personal
soumrak *n.* dusk
soused *n.* neighbor
spadnout *v.* fall
spát *v.* sleep
specifický *adj.* particular
spěch *n.* hurry
spisovatel *n.* writer
spojení *n.* union; alliance
spojit *v.* combine; join
spojka *n. gram.* conjunction
společenský *adj.* social
společnost *n.* company
spolu *adv.* along
spor *n.* dispute
správa *n.* administration
spravedlivý *adj.* fair
spravedlnost *n.* justice
správný *adj.* correct
spropitné *n.* tip; fee
srazit se *v.* collide
srdce *n.* heart
srovnat *v.* compare
srpen *n.* August
stálý *n.* permanent
stanice *n.* station
stanovisko *n.* attitude

starost *n.* care; concern
starý *adj.* old; ancient
stát *n.* state; country
stát *v.* stand
statek *n.* farm
stát se *v.* happen; become
stavba *n.* construction
stejný *adj.* same; equal
stěna *n.* wall
stěžovat si *v.* complain
stín *n.* shadow
stipendium *n.* grant
století *n.* century
strana *n.* page; side
stroj *n.* machine
strom *n.* tree
strop *n.* ceiling
střed *n.* center
středa *n.* Wednesday
střední *adj.* middle
střecha *n.* roof
střela *n.* bullet
studovat *v.* study
stůl *n.* table
stupeň *n.* degree
stvrzenka *n.* receipt
sucho *n.* drought
suchý *adj.* dry
sůl *n.* salt
sušenka *n.* cookie; biscuit
suterén *n.* basement
svátek *n.* holiday
svázat *v.* bind
svazek *n.* alliance
svět *n.* world
světlo *n.* light
svetr *n.* sweater

svítání *n.* sunrise
svoboda *n.* freedom
svobodný *adj.* free
svobodný muž *n.* bachelor
syn *n.* son
sýr *n.* cheese
syrový *adj.* raw

Š

šachta *n.* mine
šachy *n.* chess
šálek *n.* cup
šampaňské *n.* champagne
šance *n.* chance
šaty *n.* dress
šedý *adj.* gray
šest *num.* six
široký *adj.* wide
škola *n.* school
špatně *adv.* badly
špatný *adj.* bad
špenát *n.* spinach
špína *n.* dirt
špinavý *adj.* dirty
šplhat *v.* climb
šťastný *adj.* happy; lucky
šunka *n.* ham
švestka *n.* plum

T

tabák *n.* tobacco
tabletka *n.* pill
tábor *n.* camp

tak *adv.* so
také *adv.* also
takový *adj.* such
talíř *n.* plate
tam *adv.* there
tanec *n.* dance
taneční sál *n.* ballroom
taška *n.* bag
taxi *n.* cab
teď *adv.* now
telecí maso *n.* veal
telefon *n.* phone
tělo *n.* body
téměř *adv.* almost
tenký *adj.* thin
teplo *n.* heat
teplota *n.* temperature
teplý *adj.* warm
těšit se *v.* enjoy
těžce *adv.* heavily
těžký *adj.* heavy; difficult
tichý *adj.* quiet
tisk *n.* press
tkanina *n.* texture
tlačit *v.* push
tlak *n.* pressure
tlustý *adj.* fat
tmavý *adj.* black; dark
to *pron.* that
toaleta *n.* toilet
toaletní papír *n.* toilet paper
toho *adv.* besides
topinka *n.* toast
továrna *n.* factory
tradice *n.* tradition
tramvaj *n.* tram; streetcar
tráva *n.* grass

trh *n.* market
trouba *n.* oven
trpký *adj.* bitter
trvat *v.* insist; last
třešeň *n.* cherry
tři *num.* three
třída *n.* category
tuhý papír *n.* card
tužka *n.* pencil
tvar *n.* form
tvář *n.* cheek
tvrdý *adj.* hard
tvůj; **váš**; **svůj** (**tvoje**; **vaše**; **vaši**) *adj.* your
tvůj; **váš** *pron.* yours
ty; **vy** *pron.* you
tyč *n.* bar
týden *n.* week
tykev *n.* pumpkin

U

u *prep.* at; by
ubytování *n.* accommodation
ubytovat *v.* house
úcta *n.* respect
účast *n.* presence
učení *n.* instruction
účet *n.* bill; account; invoice
učit *v.* teach
učitel *n.* teacher
učit se *v.* learn
událost *n.* incident; event
uhlí *n.* coal
uhodit *v.* hit; knock
ucho *n.* ear
ujistit *v.* assure

ukazovat *v.* show
úklid *n.* cleaning
ulehčit *v.* facilitate
ulice *n.* street
umělec *n.* artist
umění *n.* art
umět *v.* can
/u/mlít *v.* grind
úmysl *n.* intention; aim
umývadlo *n.* basin; sink
únava *n.* fatigue
unavený *adj.* tired
univerzita *n.* university
únor *n.* February
úplně *adv.* completely
upomínka *n.* demand
určení *n.* appointment
určit *v.* determine
určitě *adv.* definitely
určitý *adj.* specific; certain
úroveň *n.* standard; level
urovnat *v.* arrange
úřední *adj.* official
úředník *n.* official
usadit se *v.* settle
/u/schovat *v.* hide
úsměv *n.* smile
úspěch *n.* success; achievement
úspěšný *adj.* successful
uspořádání *n.* arrangement
ústa *n. pl.* mouth
ústav *n.* institute
útěk *n.* escape
úterý *n.* Tuesday
útok *n.* attack
utrácet *v.* spend
utváření *n.* formation

/u/tvořit /se/ *v.* form
/u/vařit *v.* cook
uvažovat *v.* contemplate
uvědomit si *v.* realize
úvěr *n.* credit
uvnitř *adv.* inside
úvod *n.* introduction
úzký *adj.* narrow
už *adv.* yet; already
užít *v.* use
užitečný *adj.* useful

V

v *prep.* in
váha *n.* balance; weight
vajíčko *n.* egg
válka *n.* war
vana *n.* bathtub
varieté *n.* variety
varovat *v.* warn
vařit *v.* boil
váza *n.* vase
vázat *v.* bind
vážný *adj.* serious
včela *n.* bee
včera *adv.* yesterday
včetně *prep.* including
vděčný *adj.* grateful
věc *n.* thing; article
večer *n.* evening
večeře *n.* dinner; supper
večeřet *v.* dine
večírek *n.* party
věda *n.* science
vědět *v.* know

vedle *prep.* near
vedoucí *n.* chief; leader
vědro *n.* bucket
věk *n.* age; era
Velikonoce *n.* Easter
velikost *n.* size
velký *adj.* big; large; great
velmi *adv.* very
venkovský *adj.* rural
venku *adv.* outside; out
věnovat *v.* devote
vepřové maso *n.* pork
věřejný *adj.* public
věřitel *n.* creditor
vesnice *n.* village
vést *v.* guide
větev (stromu) *n.* branch
věznice *n.* prison
věž *n.* tower
vhodný *adj.* suitable
vchod *n.* gate; entry
více *adv.* more
vidět *v.* see
víkend *n.* weekend
vina *n.* blame
víno *n.* wine
vítat *v.* welcome
vítězství *n.* victory
vítr *n.* wind
vklad *n.* deposit
vláda *n.* government
vlajka *n.* flag
vlak *n.* train
vlastně *adv.* actually
vlastní *adj.* own; proper
vlastnit *v.* own
vlasy *n.* hair

vlašský ořech *n.* walnut
vliv *n.* influence
vlna *n.* wool
vlna (na vodě) *n.* wave (on the water)
vnitřní *adj.* inner; internal
voda *n.* water
voják *n.* soldier
volit *v.* vote
volný *adj.* free
vonět *v.* smell
vosa *n.* wasp
vousy *n. pl.* beard
v podstatě *adv.* basically
vpřed *adv.* ahead; along
vpustit *v.* admit
vřelý *adj.* boiling
vskutku *adv.* indeed
vstoupit *v.* come in
však *adv.* however
/vše/obecný *adj.* general
všichni *adj.* all
vůbec *adv.* at all
vůz *n.* car; vehicle; carriage
výběr *n.* choice; digest
vybrat *v.* choose
vydání *n.* edition; publication; emission
vydat *v.* publish; issue
výhled *n.* view
vyhnout se *v.* avoid
výhoda *n.* advantage
východ *n.* exit; east
výchova *n.* education
vychovávat *v.* educate
výjimka *n.* exception
/vy/kopat *v.* dig
výměna *n.* change; exchange

vyměnit *v.* barter
vymyslet *v.* fabricate
vynikající *adj.* excellent
vypínač *n.* switch
výpočet *n.* calculation
vyrábět *v.* generate
výrobek *n.* product
vyrušit *v.* disturb
/vy/řešení *n.* solution
výsledek *n.* outcome
vysoce *adv.* highly
vysoká škola *n.* college
vysoký *adj.* tall; high
výstava *n.* exhibition; display
vysvětlení *n.* interpretation
vysvětlit *v.* explain
vysvětlovat *v.* interpret
vyšetřit *v.* investigate
vyšetřování *n.* investigation
výška *n.* height
výtah *n.* elevator
vytvoření *n.* institution
vyzdobit *v.* decorate
výzkum *n.* research; meaning
výzva *n.* appeal
vyžadovat *v.* require
výživa *n.* diet
vzbudit se *v.* awaken
vzdálenost *n.* distance
vzduch *n.* air
vzhled *n.* aspect
vzít *v.* take; pick
vzor *n.* design
vzpomenout si *v.* remember
vztah *n.* relationship
vždy *adv.* always

Z

z *prep.* from; off
za *prep.* behind
zabalit *v.* wrap
zábava *n.* entertainment
zabít *v.* kill
zabránit *v.* prevent
záclona *n.* curtain
začít *v.* begin; start
záda *n.* back (of body)
zadní sedadlo *n.* back
zahanbený *adj.* ashamed
zahrada *n.* garden
zahrnout *v.* include; incorporate
záhyb *n.* fold
záchod *n.* toilet
zachránit *v.* save
zájem *n.* interest; behalf
zajímat se *v.* interested
zajímavý *adj.* interesting
zajít pro *v.* fetch
zájmeno *n. gram.* pronoun
zajmout *v.* capture
zákaz *n.* ban
zakázat *v.* forbid
základní *adj.* fundamental; primary; basic
/za/klepání *n.* knock
zákon *n.* law
záležitost *n.* issue; affair; matter
založení *n.* foundation
zámek *n.* castle; lock
zaměřit se *v.* focus
zaměstnání *n.* employment; business
zamířit *v.* aim
zamknout *v.* lock
západ *n.* west

západ slunce *n.* sunset
zápalka *n.* match
/za/parkovat *v.* park
/za/píchnout *v.* stick
/za/platit *v.* pay
zapojit *v.* involve
zapomenout *v.* forget
záporný *adj.* negative
záruka *n.* bail
září *n.* September
zasnoubený *adj.* engaged
zastavit *v.* stop
zastávka *n.* stop
zástupce *n.* agent
zatáčka *n.* bend
/za/tahnout *v.* pull
záviset *v.* depend
/za/volání *n.* call
/za/volat *v.* call
závrať *n.* vertigo
zavřít *v.* shut
záznam *n.* record
záznamenat *v.* register
zdatnost *n.* ability
zdát se *v.* seem
zde *adv.* here
zdraví *n.* health
zelenina *n.* vegetable
zelený *adj.* green
země *n.* country, land; earth, ground
zima *n.* winter
zisk *n.* profit
získat *v.* acquire; gain
zítra *adv.* tomorrow
zjevný *adj.* apparent
zklamat *v.* disappoint
zkouška *n.* examination

zkusit *v.* try
zlato *n.* gold
zlepšení *n.* improvement
zlepšit *v.* improve
zlomit *v.* break
změna *n.* change; variation
změnit *v.* alter
zmenšit *v.* reduce
zmeškat *v.* miss
zmínit se *v.* mention
zmizet *v.* disappear
značka *n.* mark
znalost *n.* skill; knowledge
znamenat *v.* mean
zničit *v.* destroy
znovu *adv.* again; anew
zoologická zahrada *n.* zoo
zotavit se *v.* recover
zpětný *adj.* backward
zpěvák *n.* singer
zpívat *v.* sing
zpoždění *n.* delay
zpracování *n.* processing
zpráva *n.* news; message; report
zrak *n.* vision
zranění *n.* injury
zrcadlo *n.* mirror
zrušit *v.* cancel
zřejmě *adv.* apparently
zřejmý *adj.* obvious
ztráta *n.* loss
ztratit *v.* lose; disappear
zub *n.* tooth
zubní *adj.* dental
zubní lékař *n.* dentist
zuby *n. pl.* teeth
zůstat *v.* stay

zvěrokruh *n.* zodiac
zvěřina *n.* venison
zvíře *n.* animal
zvítězit *v.* win
zvládnout *v.* manage
zvláštní *adj.* exceptional
zvon *n.* bell
zvracet *v.* vomit
zvýšení *n.* increase
zvýšit *v.* increase
zvyšující se *adj.* increasing

Ž

žádný *pron.* neither; no
žádost *n.* application; appeal
žárlivost *n.* jealousy
žebřík *n.* ladder
žehlit *v.* iron
železnice *n.* railroad
žena *n.* woman
ženský *adj.* female
židle *n.* chair; seat
žijící *adj.* alive
žíla *n.* vein
život *n.* life
životopis *n.* biography
žízeň *n.* thirst
žloutek *n.* yolk
žlutý *adj.* yellow
žvýkat *v.* chew

ENGLISH-CZECH DICTIONARY

A

abandon *v.* opustit
ability *n.* zdatnost
able *adj.* schopný
aboard *adv.* na palubě
about *adv.* asi
above *adv.* nahoře
absence *n.* nepřítomnost
absolutely *adv.* naprosto
academic *adj.* akademický
accept *v.* přijmout
access *n.* přístup
accident *n.* nehoda
accommodation *n.* ubytování
accompany *v.* doprovodit
according *prep.* podle
account *n.* účet; konto
account *v.* odpovídat (za něco)
accuse *v.* obžalovat
achieve *v.* dosáhnout
achievement *n.* úspěch
acid *n.* kyselina
acknowledge *v.* přiznat
acquire *v.* získat
across *prep.* přes
act *n.* čin
action *n.* činnost
active *adj.* aktivní
activity *n.* aktivita
actual *adj.* skutečný

actually *adv.* vlastně; opravdu
add *v.* dodat, přidat
addition *n.* přidání
addition *n.* dodatek
additional *adj.* doplňkový
address *n.* adresa
adjective *n. gram.* podstatné jméno
administration *n.* správa
admire *v.* obdivovat se
admit *v.* vpustit; připustit
adopt *v.* adoptovat
adult *adj.* dospělý
advance *n.* postup
advantage *n.* výhoda
adverb *n. gram.* příslovce
advice *n.* rada
advise *v.* poradit
affair *n.* záležitost
affect *v.* působit
afford *v.* dovolit si
afraid *v.* bát se
after *adv.* pak, potom
afternoon *n.* odpoledne
afterwards *adv.* potom
again *adv.* znovu, opět
against *prep.* proti, naproti
age *n.* věk
agency *n.* jednatelství; kancelář; agentura
agenda *n.* program
agent *n.* zástupce
ago *adv.* před
agree *v.* souhlasit
agreement *n.* souhlas
ahead *adv.* vpřed; napřed
aid *n.* pomoc
aim *n.* úmysl; cíl
aim *v.* zamířit

air *n.* vzduch
airplane *n.* letadlo
airport *n.* letiště
alike *adj.* podobný
alive *adj.* žijící
all *adj.* všichni
alliance *n.* spojení, svazek
allow *v.* dovolit, povolit
almost *adv.* téměř, skoro
alone *adj.* sám
along *adv.* vpřed; spolu
along *prep.* po
aloud *adv.* nahlas
alphabet *n.* abeceda
already *adv.* už
also *adv.* rovněž, také
alter *v.* změnit
alternative *adj.* alternativní
although *conj.* ačkoli
always *adv.* vždy
A.M. *n.* dopoledne
ambulance *n.* sanitka
American *adj.* americký
American *n.* Američan
among *prep.* mezi
amount *n.* částka
analysis *n.* analýza, rozbor (krve)
analyze *v.* analyzovat
ancient *adj.* starý
and *conj.* a; i
anew *adv.* opět, znovu
angry *adj.* rozhněvaný
animal *n.* zvíře
announce *v.* oznámit, ohlásit
annual *adj.* roční
another *adj.* další
answer *n.* odpověď

answer *v.* odpovědět
any *adj.* nějaký
anybody *pron.* někdo
anything *pron.* něco
anywhere *adv.* kdekoli
apart *adv.* odděleně
apartment *n.* byt
apparent *adj.* zjevný
apparently *adv.* zřejmě
appeal *n.* žádost; výzva
appeal *v.* apelovat (na); obrátit se
apple *n.* jablko
application *n.* žádost
apply *v.* požádat
appoint *v.* jmenovat
appointment *n.* určení; schůzka; čas
appreciate *v.* oceňovat
approach *n.* přiblížení, příchod
appropriate *adj.* patřičný
approve *v.* schvalovat
apricot *n.* meruňka
April *n.* duben
area *n.* plocha
argue *v.* diskutovat
argument *n.* důvod
arm *n.* ruka
army *n.* armáda
around *adv.* okolo, kolem
arrange *v.* urovnat
arrangement *n.* uspořádání
arrival *n.* příchod
arrive *v.* přijít
art *n.* umění
article *n.* věc
artist *n.* umělec
as *adv.* jako
as *conj.* když

ash *n.* popel
ashamed *adj.* zahanbený
ask *v.* ptát se, zeptat se
aspect *n.* vzhled
aspiration *n.* snaha
assembly *n.* shromáždění
assent *n.* souhlas
assess *v.* ohodnotit
asset *n.* přínos
assistance *n.* pomoc
associate *v.* sdružovat
association *n.* organizace
assume *v.* předpokládat
assumption *n.* předpoklad
assure *v.* ujistit
at *prep.* na, u
at all *adv.* vůbec
atmosphere *n.* ovzduší
attach *v.* připevnit
attack *n.* útok
attack *v.* napadnout
attempt *n.* pokus
attention *n.* pozornost
attitude *n.* stanovisko
attractive *adj.* přitažlivý
audience *n.* posluchači
August *n.* srpen
author *n.* autor
authority *n.* pravomoc
autumn *n.* podzim
available *adj.* přístupný
avoid *v.* vyhnout se
await *v.* čekat
awaken *v.* vzbudit se
award *n.* cena
away *adv.* pryč

B

baby *n.* děťátko
bachelor *n.* svobodný muž
back *n.* záda
backbite *v.* pomlouvat
backbone *n.* páteř
back seat *n.* zadní sedadlo
backward *adj.* zpětný
bacon *n.* slanina
bacteria *n.* bakterie
bad *adj.* špatný
badly *adv.* špatně
bag *n.* taška
bail *n.* záruka
bake *v.* péci
baker *n.* pekař
bakery *n.* pekárna
baking *n.* pečení
balance *n.* váha
balcony *n.* balkón
baldly *adv.* rovnou, otevřeně
ball *n.* míč
ballroom *n.* taneční sál
ban *n.* zákaz
banal *adj.* banální
banana *n.* banán
bangle *n.* náramek
bank *n.* banka
banking *n.* bankovnictví
banknote *n.* bankovka
banquet *n.* recepce
bar *n.* tyč
barbecue *n.* piknik
barber *n.* holič
bargain *n.* obchodní dohoda
baroque *adj.* barokní

barter *v.* vyměnit
basement *n.* suterén
basic *adj.* základní; elementární
basically *adv.* v podstatě, v zásadě
basin *n.* umývadlo
bask *v.* slunit se
basketball *n.* košíková
bath *n.* koupel
bathe *v.* koupat se
bathroom *n.* koupelna
bathtub *n.* vana
be *v.* být
beach *n.* pláž
bean *n.* fazole
beard *n.* brada; vousy
beautiful *adj.* krásný
because *conj.* protože
become *v.* stát se (jakým; čím)
bed *n.* postel
bedclothes *n. pl.* ložní prádlo
bedroom *n.* ložnice; pokoj (v hotelu)
bee *n.* včela
beef *n.* hovězí maso
beer *n.* pivo
before *prep.* před
begin *v.* začít; otevřít
behalf *n.* zájem
behind *prep.* za
bell *n.* zvon
belong *v.* patřit
beloved *adj.* drahý
below *adv.* dolů; níže
bench *n.* lavička
bend *n.* ohyb; zatáčka
besides *adv.* kromě toho
best *adj.* nejlepší

between *prep.* mezi
beverage *n.* nápoj
bicycle *n.* kolo
big *adj.* velký
bill *n.* účet
bill (**currency**) *n.* bankovka
billiards *n.* kulečník
bind *v.* svázat, vázat
binder *n.* knihař
binoculars *n.* dalekohled
biography *n.* životopis
bird *n.* pták
birth *n.* narození
birthday *n.* narozeniny
biscuit *n.* sušenka, keks
bit *n.* kousek
bitter *adj.* trpký, hořký
black *adj.* černý, tmavý
blame *n.* vina, obviňování
blanket *n.* deka
bleed *v.* krvácet
blink *n.* mrknutí
blood *n.* krev
bloom *n.* květ
blouse *n.* halenka
blue *adj.* modrý
board *n.* deska
boat *n.* loďka
body *n.* tělo
Bohemia *n.* Čechy
Bohemian *adj.* český
boil *v.* vařit
boiling *adj.* vřelý
book *n.* kniha
bookcase *n.* knihovna
born *adj.* narozen
bottle *n.* láhev

bouquet *n.* kytice
box *n.* krabice
boy *n.* chlapec
brag *v.* chvástat se
branch *n.* větev /stromu/
bracelet *n.* náramek
bread *n.* chléb
break *v.* rozbít; zlomit
breakfast *n.* snídaně
breast *n.* prsa
breath *n.* dech
brick *n.* cihla
bridge *n.* most
bring *v.* přinést
brother *n.* bratr
brown *adj.* hnědý
brush *n.* kartáč
bucket *n.* kbelík, vědro
build *v.* postavit
bullet *n.* střela
bus *n.* autobus
business *n.* zaměstnání
but *conj.* ale
butter *n.* máslo
butterfly *n.* motýl
button *n.* knoflík
buy *v.* koupit
by *prep.* u; k; vedle
bye *interj.* ahoj

C

cab *n.* taxi
cafe *n.* kavárna
cafeteria *n.* kantýna
cake *n.* koláč

calculation *n.* výpočet
calendar *n.* kalendář
call *n.* /za/volání
call *v.* /za/volat
camera *n.* fotoaparát
camp *n.* tábor
can *v.* moci; umět
cancel *v.* odvolat, zrušit
candy *n.* bonbón
cap *n.* čepice
capital *n.* hlavní město
captain *n.* kapitán
capture *v.* zajmout, dopadnout
car *n.* vůz, auto
card *n.* tuhý papír, kartón
care *n.* starost, péče
care *v.* pečovat
carnation *n.* karafiát
carriage *n.* vůz, kočár
carrot *n.* mrkev
carry *v.* nést, nosit
carton *n.* krabiče
case *n.* případ
cash *n.* peníze
cashier *n.* pokladník
castle *n.* hrad, zámek
cat *n.* kočka
catch *v.* chytat
category *n.* třída
Catholic *adj.* katolický
cauliflower *n.* květák
cause *n.* příčina
cautious *adj.* obezřetelný, opatrný
cave *n.* jeskyně
caviar *n.* kaviár
cease *v.* přestat
ceiling *n.* strop

celebrate *v.* slavit
celery *n.* celer
cement *n.* cement
cent *n.* cent
center *n.* střed
central *adj.* centrální
century *n.* století
cereal *n.* obilovina
ceremony *n.* obřad, slavnost
certain *adj.* jistý, určitý
certificate *n.* osvědčení
certify *v.* potvrdit
chain *n.* řetěz
chair *n.* židle
chalk *n.* křída
chamber *n.* komnata
champagne *n.* šampaňské
chance *n.* šance, možnost
change *n.* změna; výměna
chapter *n.* kapitola
charcoal *n.* dřevěné uhlí
charm *n.* půvab
chauffeur *n.* řidič
cheap *adj.* levný
check *n.* kontrola
cheek *n.* tvář
cheers *interj.* na zdraví
cheese *n.* sýr
cherry *n.* třešeň
chess *n.* šachy
chew *v.* žvýkat
chicken *n.* kuře
chief *n.* vedoucí
child *n.* dítě
chill *n.* chlad
chimney *n.* komín
chin *n.* brada

china *n.* porcelán
chives *n.* pažitka
chocolate *n.* čokoláda
choice *n.* výběr
choose *v.* vybrat
church *n.* kostel
cigar *n.* doutník
cigarette *n.* cigareta
cinema *n.* kino
cinnamon *n.* skořice
circle *n.* kruh
citizen *n.* občan
city *n.* město
clap *v.* potleskat
clean *adj.* čistý
cleaning *n.* úklid
clear *adj.* čirý
clever *adj.* chytrý
climb *v.* šplhat
clinic *n.* klinika
clock *n.* hodiny
close *adj.* blízký
clothes *n.* oblečení
cloud *n.* mrak
coal *n.* uhlí
coat *n.* kabát
cocoa *n.* kakao
coconut *n.* kokos
coffee *n.* káva
cognition *n.* poznání
coin *n.* mince
cold *n.* chlad
collar *n.* límec
collect *v.* sbírat
college *n.* vysoká škola; kolej
collide *v.* srazit se
color *n.* barva

comb *n.* hřeben
combine *v.* spojit
come *v.* přijít
come in *v.* vstoupit
command *v.* přikázat; ovládat
company *n.* společnost
compare *v.* srovnat
complain *v.* stěžovat si
completely *adv.* úplně
computer *n.* počítač
concern *n.* starost
concert *n.* koncert
confectionery *n.* cukroví
confirmed *adj.* potvrzený
congratulate *v.* blahopřát
conjunction *n. gram.* spojka
construction *n.* stavba
contain *v.* obsahovat
contemplate *v.* uvažovat
continue *v.* pokračovat
contract *n.* smlouva
converse *v.* hovořit
cook *v.* /u/vařit
cookie *n.* sušenka
cool *adj.* chladný
copy *n.* kopie
corn *n.* kukuřice
correct *adj.* správný
corridor *n.* chodba
cost *n.* cena
costly *adj.* drahý
cotton *n.* bavlna
cough *n.* kašel
country *n.* země, stát
cover *n.* poklice
cream *n.* smetana
credit *n.* úvěr, kredit

creditor *n.* věřitel
cricket *n.* kriket
critical *adj.* kritický
croquet *n.* kroket
cruel *adj.* krutý
cry *n.* křik; pláč
crystal *n.* krystal
cucumber *n.* okurka
cultural *adj.* kulturní
cup *n.* šálek
cure *n.* léčba
curry *n.* kari
curtain *n.* záclona
cut *n.* říznutí; kousek
cut *v.* říznout
cute *adj.* roztomilý
cutlet *n.* kotleta
Czech *adj.* český

D

daily *adj.* denní
dairy *n.* mlékárna
dam *n.* přehrada
damage *n.* poškození
dance *n.* tanec
dandruff *n.* lupy
danger *n.* nebezpečí
dark *adj.* tmavý
darling *n.* miláček
date *n.* datum
day *n.* den
deadline *n.* konečný termín
deal *n.* dohoda
dear *adj.* drahý
debate *n.* debata, diskuse

debt *n.* dluh
December *n.* prosinec
decide *v.* rozhodnout /se/
decorate *v.* vyzdobit
decrease *n.* snížení
deep *adj.* hluboký
deeply *adv.* hluboce
defeat *n.* porážka; prohra
defect *n.* nedostatek
defend *v.* bránit
definitely *adv.* určitě
degree *n.* stupeň
delay *n.* zpoždění
demand *n.* požadavek; upomínka
dental *adj.* zubní
dentist *n.* zubní lékař
deny *v.* popřít
depart *v.* odjet
departure *n.* odchod
depend *v.* záviset
deposit *n.* vklad
depth *n.* hloubka
descend *v.* sestupovat
descent *n.* sestup
design *n.* vzor
designate *v.* označit
designer *n.* návrhář
desk *n.* psací stůl; lavice
dessert *n.* moučník
destroy *v.* zničit
detail *n.* detail
determine *v.* určit
develop *v.* rozvinout
devote *v.* věnovat
dew *n.* rosa
diaper *n.* plenka
diarrhea *n.* průjem

diary *n.* deník
dictionary *n.* slovník
diet *n.* výživa; dieta
difference *n.* rozdíl
difficult *adj.* těžký
dig *v.* /vy/kopat
digest *n.* výběr
dignify *v.* poctít
dignity *n.* důstojnost
dine *v.* večeřet
dinner *n.* večeře
direct *adj.* přímý
director *n.* ředitel
dirt *n.* špína
dirty *adj.* špinavý
disagree *v.* nesouhlasit
disappear *v.* zmizet, ztratit se
disappoint *v.* zklamat
discount *n.* sleva
discover *v.* objevit
discuss *v.* jednat
dish *n.* mísa
diskette *n.* disketa
dislike *n.* odpor
disperse *v.* rozehnat
display *n.* výstavka
dispute *n.* polemika; spor
dissolve *v.* rozpustit se
distance *n.* vzdálenost
disturb *v.* rušit; vyrušit
divide *v.* dělit se
divorce *n.* rozvod
do *v.* dělat
doctor *n.* lékař
dog *n.* pes
doll *n.* panenka
domestic *adj.* domácí

donate *v.* darovat
door *n.* dveře
dormitory *n.* kolej
double *adj.* dvojitý
down *adv.* dolů
downtown *n.* centrum města
draw *v.* kreslit
drawing *n.* kreslení
dream *n.* sen
dress *n.* šaty
drink *n.* nápoj
drink *v.* pít
drinking *n.* pití
drive *n.* jízda, cesta
driver *n.* řidič
drop *n.* kapka
drought *n.* sucho
drug *n.* lék
drugstore *n.* lékárna
drunk *adj.* opilý
dry *adj.* suchý
dumpling *n.* knedlík
during *prep.* během
dusk *n.* soumrak
dust *n.* prach
duty *n.* povinnost

E

each *adj.* každý
ear *n.* ucho
earring *n.* náušnice
earth *n.* země
east *n.* východ
Easter *n.* Velikonoce
easy *adj.* lehký

eat *v.* jíst
edge *n.* okraj
edition *n.* vydání
educate *v.* vychovávat
education *n.* výchova
egg *n.* vajíčko
eight *num.* osm
either *adj.* jeden
elastic *adj.* pružný
electricity *n.* elektřina
electronics *n.* elektronika
elegant *adj.* elegantní
elevator *n.* výtah
else *adj.* jiný
e-mail *n.* elektronická pošta
embark *v.* nalodit se
emission *n.* vydání
employment *n.* zaměstnání
empty *adj.* prázdný
enclose *v.* obehnat
encourage *v.* povzbuzovat
end *n.* konec
energy *n.* energie
engage *v.* najmout
engaged *adj.* zasnoubený
English *adj.* anglický
enjoy *v.* těšit se
enough *adv.* dost
entertainment *n.* zábava
entire *adj.* celý
entry *n.* vchod, příjezd
envelope *n.* obálka
equal *adj.* stejný
era *n.* věk
escape *n.* útěk
esplanade *n.* promenáda
evaluate *v.* ocenit

even *adj.* rovný
evening *n.* večer
event *n.* událost
every *adj.* každý
everyday *adj.* každodenní
evidence *n.* důkaz
examination *n.* zkouška
example *n.* příklad
excellent *adj.* vynikající
except *prep.* kromě
exception *n.* výjimka
exceptional *adj.* zvláštní
exchange *n.* výměna
exhibition *n.* výstava
exit *n.* východ
expect *v.* očekávat
expensive *adj.* drahý
expert *n.* odborník
explain *v.* vysvětlit
extra *adj.* navíc
extraordinary *adj.* mimořádný
eye *n.* oko
eyedrops *n. pl.* oční kapky

F

fable *n.* bajka
fabricate *v.* vymyslet
face *n.* obličej
facilitate *v.* ulehčit
fact *n.* skutečnost
factory *n.* továrna
fad *n.* módní výstřelek
fail *v.* selhat
faint *adj.* slabý
fair *adj.* spravedlivý

faith *n.* důvěra
fall *n.* pád
fall *v.* spadnout
fall (autumn) *n.* podzim
fame *n.* sláva
family *n.* rodina
famine *n.* hlad
famous *adj.* proslulý
fan *n.* fanda
far *adv.* daleko
faraway *adj.* daleký
farewell *n.* rozloučení
farm *n.* statek
farmer *n.* rolník
farther *adv.* dále
fashion *n.* móda
fast *adj.* rychlý
fat *adj.* tlustý
father *n.* otec
fatigue *n.* únava
feast *n.* hostina
February *n.* únor
fee *n.* spropitné
feed *n.* krmení
feel *n.* pocit
feeling *n.* hmat, cit
fellowship *n.* přátelství
female *adj.* ženský
female *n.* samice
fence *n.* plot, ohrada
festive *adj.* slavnostní
fetch *v.* zajít pro
fever *n.* horečka
few *adv.* málo
fiction *n.* beletrie
field *n.* pole
fight *n.* rvačka

fight *v.* rvát se
figure *n.* čislo
fill *v.* naplnit
film *n.* film
final *adj.* konečný
finally *adv.* konečně
finance *n.* finance
find *v.* najít
fine *adj.* pěkný
finger *n.* prst
finish *n.* konec
fire *n.* oheň
firm *adj.* pevný
firm *n.* podnik
first *adj.* první
fish *n.* ryba
fit *v.* padnout
five *num.* pět
fix *v.* pevnit
flag *n.* vlajka
flat *adj.* rovný
flesh *n.* maso
flight *n.* let
floor *n.* podlaha
flour *n.* mouka
flow *n.* proud
flower *n.* květina
fly *v.* létat
foam *n.* pěna
focus *v.* zaměřit se
fog *n.* mlha
fold *n.* záhyb
folk *n.* lidé
follow *v.* následovat
following *adj.* následující
food *n.* jídlo
foot *n.* noha

for *prep.* pro
forbid *v.* zakázat
force *n.* síla
force *v.* přinutit
forehead *n.* čelo
foreign *adj.* cizí
forest *n.* les
forever *adv.* navždy
forget *v.* zapomenout
forgive *v.* odpustit
form *n.* tvar
form *v.* /u/tvořit /se/
formal *adj.* oficiální
formation *n.* utváření
former *adj.* dřivější
forward *adv.* dopředu
foundation *n.* založení
four *num.* čtyři
frame *n.* konstrukce
free *adj.* svobodný, volný
freedom *n.* svoboda
frequently *adv.* mnohdy
fresh *adj.* čerstvý
Friday *n.* pátek
friend *n.* přítel
friendly *adj.* přátelský
friendship *n.* přátelství
from *prep.* z
front *adj.* přední
front *n.* předek
fruit *n.* ovoce
fry *v.* /o/smažit
full *adj.* plný
fully *adv.* plně
function *n.* funkce
fund *n.* fond
fundamental *adj.* základní

funny *adj.* legrační
further *adj.* další
future *adj.* budoucí
future *n.* budoucnost

G

gain *v.* získat
game *n.* hra
gap *n.* díra
garage *n.* garáž
garbage *n.* odpadky
garden *n.* zahrada
gas *n.* plyn
gasoline *n.* benzín
gate *n.* brána; vchod
gather *v.* shromáždit
general *adj.* /vše/obecný
general *n.* generál
generally *adv.* obecně
generate *v.* vyrábět
generation *n.* generace
gentleman *n.* kavalír
get *v.* dostat
gift *n.* dar
girl *n.* dívka
give *v.* dát
glad *adj.* potěšený
glance *v.* podívat se
glass *n.* sklo
glove *n.* rukavice
glue *n.* lepidlo
go *v.* jít
goal *n.* branka
gold *n.* zlato
good *adj.* dobrý

good *n.* dobro
Gothic *adj.* gotický
goulash *n.* guláš
government *n.* vláda
grammatical *adj.* gramatický
grant *n.* stipendium
grant *v.* poskytnout
grape *n.* hroznové zrnko
grass *n.* tráva
grateful *adj.* vděčný
gravy *n.* omáčka
gray *adj.* šedý
greasy *adj.* mastný
great *adj.* velký
green *adj.* zelený
greeting *n.* pozdrav
grill *v.* grilovat
grind *v.* /u/mlít
groceries *n. pl.* potraviny
ground *n.* země
group *n.* skupina
grow *v.* pěstovat
growth *n.* růst
guard *n.* hlídka
guest *n.* návštěvník
guide *n.* průvodce
guide *v.* vést
guy *n.* kluk

H

hair *n.* vlasy
half *n.* půlka
hall *n.* předsíň
ham *n.* šunka
hand *n.* ruka

handbag *n.* kabelka
handkerchief *n.* kapesník
hang *v.* pověsit
happen *v.* stát se
happy *adj.* šťastný
hard *adj.* tvrdý
hard *adv.* pilně
hardly *adv.* sotva
hat *n.* klobouk
hate *v.* nenávidět
have *v.* mít
have lunch *v.* obědvat
he *pron.* on
head *n.* hlava
head *v.* být v čele
heal *v.* hojit se
health *n.* zdraví
hear *v.* slyšet
heart *n.* srdce
heat *n.* teplo
heavily *adv.* těžce
heavy *adj.* těžký
height *n.* výška
hello *interj.* ahoj
help *n.* pomoc
help *v.* pomoci
her *pron.* ji
here *adv.* zde
hide *v.* /u/schovat
high *adj.* vysoký
highly *adv.* vysoce
hill *n.* kopec
his *pron.* jeho
historic *adj.* historický
history *n.* historie
hit *v.* uhodit
hold *v.* držet

hole *n.* díra
holiday *n.* svátek
home *n.* dům
honey *n.* med
hope *n.* naděje
hope *v.* doufat
horse *n.* kůn
hospital *n.* nemocnice
hot *adj.* horký
hotel *n.* hotel
hour *n.* hodina
house *n.* dům
house *v.* ubytovat
household *n.* domácnost
how *adv.* jak
however *adv.* však
huge *adj.* ohromný
human *adj.* lidský
hunger *n.* hlad
hurry *n.* spěch
husband *n.* manžel

I

I *pron.* já
ice *n.* led
idea *n.* myšlenka
identify *v.* poznat
identity *n.* identita
if *conj.* jestliže
ill *adj.* nemocný
illustrate *v.* ilustrovat
image *n.* obraz
imagine *v.* představit si
imitate *v.* napodobovat
immediate *adj.* okamžitý

immediately *adv.* okamžitě
impact *n.* náraz
imply *v.* naznačit
importance *n.* důležitost
important *adj.* důležitý
impose *v.* pověřovat
impossible *adj.* nemožný
impression *n.* dojem
improve *v.* zlepšit
improvement *n.* zlepšení
in *adv.* dovnitř
in *prep.* v, na
incident *n.* událost
include *v.* zahrnout
including *prep.* včetně
income *n.* příjem
incorporate *v.* zahrnout
increase *n.* zvýšení
increase *v.* zvýšit
increasing *adj.* zvyšující se
indeed *adv.* vskutku
independence *n.* nezávislost
independent *adj.* nezávislý
index *n.* rejstřík
indicate *v.* označit
individual *n.* jednotlivec
industrial *adj.* průmyslový
industry *n.* průmysl
inflation *n.* inflace
influence *n.* vliv
influence *v.* ovlivnit
inform *v.* informovat
information *n.* informace
initial *adj.* počáteční
initiative *n.* iniciativa
injury *n.* zranění
ink *n.* inkoust

inner *adj.* vnitřní
inquiry *n.* dotaz
insect *n.* hmyz
inside *adv.* uvnitř
insist *v.* trvat
instance *n.* případ
instead *prep.* místo
institute *n.* ústav
institution *n.* vytvoření
instruction *n.* učení
instrument *n.* nástroj
insurance *n.* pojištění
intend *v.* chtít
intention *n.* úmysl
interest *n.* zájem
interested *v.* zajímat se
interesting *adj.* zajímavý
internal *adj.* vnitřní
international *adj.* mezinárodní
interpret *v.* vysvětlovat
interpretation *n.* vysvětlení
interrupt *v.* přerušit
interview *n.* pohovor
into *prep.* do
introduce *v.* představit
introduction *n.* úvod
investigate *v.* vyšetřit
investigation *n.* vyšetřování
investment *n.* investice
invite *v.* pozvat
invoice *n.* účet
involve *v.* zapojit
iron *v.* žehlit
island *n.* ostrov
issue *n.* záležitost
issue *v.* vydat

it *pron.* to
item *n.* předmět

J

jacket *n.* sako
jam *n.* džem
January *n.* leden
jealousy *n.* žárlivost
job *n.* práce
join *v.* spojit
joint *n.* kloub
journey *n.* cesta
joy *n.* radost
judge *n.* soudce
judge *v.* soudit
July *n.* červenec
jump *v.* skákat
June *n.* červen
just *adv.* právě
justice *n.* spravedlnost

K

keep *v.* /po/nechat
kettle *n.* konvice
key *n.* klíč
kick *n.* kopnutí
kid *n.* dítě
kidney *n.* ledvina
kill *v.* zabít
kind *n.* druh
king *n.* král
kiss *n.* polibek
kitchen *n.* kuchyně

knee *n.* koleno
kneel *v.* klečet
knife *n.* nůž
knit *v.* plést
knock *n.* /za/klepání
knock *v.* uhodit
know *v.* vědět
knowledge *n.* znalost

L

labor *n.* práce
lack *n.* nedostatek
ladder *n.* žebřík
lady *n.* paní
lager *n.* ležák
lamb *n.* jehně
lamp *n.* lampa
land *n.* země
land *v.* přistát
language *n.* jazyk
large *adj.* velký
last *adj.* poslední
last *v.* trvat
late *adj.* pozdní
latter *adj.* pozdější
laugh *v.* smát se
law *n.* zákon
lawyer *n.* advokát
lay *v.* položit
lead *v.* řídit
leader *n.* vedoucí
leaf *n.* list
learn *v.* učit se
leave *v.* opustit
left *adv.* doleva

leg *n.* noha
lemon *n.* citrón
length *n.* délka
less *adv.* méně
lesson *n.* lekce
let *v.* dovolit
letter *n.* dopis
level *adj.* rovný
level *n.* úroveň
library *n.* knihovna
lie *v.* ležet
life *n.* život
lift *n.* výtah
light *n.* světlo
light *v.* rozsvítit
like *prep.* jako
like *v.* mít rád
limit *n.* hranice
line *n.* čára
link *n.* článek
lion *n.* lev
lip *n.* ret
list *n.* seznam
list *v.* sepsat
listen *v.* poslouchat
little *adv.* málo
live *v.* bydlet
liver *n.* játra
loan *n.* půjčka
local *adj.* místní
lock *n.* zámek
lock *v.* zamknout
long *adj.* dlouhý
look *n.* pohled
look *v.* dívat se
lord *n.* pán
lose *v.* ztratit

loss *n.* ztráta
love *n.* láska
love *v.* milovat
lovely *adj.* rozkošný
low *adj.* nízký
lucky *adj.* šťastný
lunch *n.* oběd
lungs *n. pl.* plíce

M

machine *n.* stroj
madam *n.* paní
magazine *n.* časopis
maid *n.* služebná
mail *n.* pošta
main *adj.* hlavní
make *v.* dělat
make an appointment *v.* objednat se (u doktora)
male *adj.* mužský
man *n.* muž
manage *v.* zvládnout
manager *n.* ředitel
manipulate *v.* manipulovat
many *adj.* mnoho
map *n.* mapa
March *n.* březen
mark *n.* značka
mark *v.* označit
market *n.* trh
marriage *n.* manželství
marry *v.* oženit se
match *n.* zápalka
material *n.* látka
matter *n.* záležitost
May *n.* květen

may *v.* moci
maybe *adv.* možná
me *pron.* mne; mě; mně; mi
meal *n.* jídlo
mean *v.* znamenat
meaning *n.* význam
meanwhile *adv.* mezitím
measure *n.* míra
meat *n.* maso
mechanic *n.* mechanik
medical *adj.* lékařský
meet *v.* potkat
meeting *n.* schůze
member *n.* člen
membership *n.* členství
mention *v.* zmínit se
message *n.* zpráva
method *n.* metoda
midday *n.* poledne
middle *adj.* střední
might *v.* mohl bych
milk *n.* mléko
mind *n.* mysl
mind *v.* dbát
mine *n.* šachta
minority *n.* menšina
minute *n.* minuta
mirror *n.* zrcadlo
Miss *n.* slečna
miss *v.* zmeškat
mistake *n.* chyba
mix *v.* smíchat
modern *adj.* moderní
Monday *n.* pondělí
money *n.* peníze
month *n.* měsíc
more *adv.* více

morning *n.* ráno
most *adv.* nejvíc
mother *n.* matka
motor *n.* motor
mountain *n.* hora
mouth *n.* ústa
move *n.* pohyb
move *v.* přestěhovat se
Mr. *n.* pán
Mrs. *n.* paní
much *adv.* mnoho
museum *n.* muzeum
mushroom *n.* houba
music *n.* hudba
must *v.* muset

N

nail *n.* nehet
name *n.* jméno
name *v.* nazvat
narrow *adj.* úzký
national *adj.* národní
natural *adj.* přírodní
nature *n.* příroda
near *prep.* vedle
nearby *adj.* nedaleký
necessary *adj.* nutný
neck *n.* krk
need *n.* nutnost
need *v.* potřebovat
needle *n.* jehla
negative *adj.* záporný
neighbor *n.* soused
neither *pron.* žadný
network *n.* síť

never *adv.* nikdy
nevertheless *adv.* nicméně
new *adj.* nový
news *n.* zpráva
newspaper *n.* noviny
next *adj.* příští
nice *adj.* pěkný
night *n.* noc
nine *num.* devět
no *adj.* žádný
no *part.* ne
nobody *pron.* nikdo
noise *n.* hluk
none *pron.* nikdo
noon *n.* poledne
normal *adj.* obvyklý
north *n.* sever
nose *n.* nos
not *part.* ne
note *n.* poznámka
note *v.* poznamenat
nothing *pron.* nic
notice *n.* oznámení
noun *n. gram.* podstatné jméno
November *n.* listopad
now *adv.* teď
nuclear *adj.* jaderný
number *n.* číslo
number *n. gram.* číslovka
nurse *n.* sestra
nut *n.* ořech

O

obey *v.* poslouchat
object *n.* předmět

obligation *n.* povinnost
observation *n.* pozorování
observe *v.* pozorovat
obtain *v.* obdržet
obvious *adj.* zřejmý
October *n.* říjen
off *adv.* pryč
off *prep.* z
offer *n.* nabídka
offer *v.* nabídnout
office *n.* kancelář
official *adj.* úřední
official *n.* úředník
often *adv.* často
oil *n.* olej
okay *interj.* fajn
old *adj.* starý
on *adv.* dál
on *prep.* na
once *adv.* jednou
one *num.* jeden
onion *n.* cibule
only *adv.* pouze
onto *prep.* směrem
open *adj.* otevřený
open *v.* otevřít
opening *n.* otevření
opinion *n.* možnost
opportunity *n.* příležitost
opposition *n.* opozice
option *n.* možnost
or *conj.* nebo
orange *adj.* oranžový
orange *n.* pomeranč
order *n.* pořadí
order *v.* nařídit
ordinary *adj.* obyčejný

organization *n.* organizace
organize *v.* organizovat
original *adj.* původní
other *adj.* další
other *pron.* jiný
otherwise *adv.* jinak
out *adv.* venku
outcome *n.* výsledek
outside *adv.* venku
oven *n.* trouba
over *prep.* nad
overtime *n.* přesčas
own *adj.* vlastní
own *v.* vlastnit
owner *n.* majitel

P

pack *v.* balit
package *n.* balík
packet *n.* balíček
page *n.* strana
pain *n.* bolest
paint *n.* barva
paint *v.* malovat
painting *n.* malba
pair *n.* pár
pan *n.* pánev
pancake *n.* palačinka
pants *n. pl.* kalhoty
paper *n.* papír
parent *n.* rodič
park *n.* park
park *v.* /za/parkovat
parking *n.* parkoviště
parliament *n.* parlament

part *n.* část
particle *n. gram.* částíce
particular *adj.* specifický
partly *adv.* částečně
partner *n.* kolega
party *n.* večírek
pass *v.* projít
passage *n.* průchod
passenger *n.* cestující
passport *n.* pas
past *adj.* minulý
past *n.* minulost
path *n.* cestička
patient *n.* nemocný
pay *n.* plat
pay *v.* /za/platit
payment *n.* placení
peace *n.* mír
peach *n.* broskev
peanut *n.* burský oříšek
pen *n.* pero
pencil *n.* tužka
people *n. pl.* lidé
perfect *adj.* dokonalý
perform *v.* provést
performance *n.* představení
perhaps *adv.* možná
period *n.* období
permanent *adj.* stálý
permit *n.* povolení
permit *v.* dovolit
person *n.* člověk
personal *adj.* soukromý
pharmacy *n.* lékárna
phone *n.* telefon
photograph *n.* fotografie
physician *n.* lékař

pick *v.* vzít
picture *n.* obraz
piece *n.* kus
pill *n.* tabletka
pillow *n.* polštář
pineapple *n.* ananas
pink *adj.* řůžový
place *n.* místo
place *v.* dát
plan *n.* plán
plan *v.* organizovat
plane *n.* letadlo
plant *n.* rostlina
plate *n.* talíř
play *n.* hra
play *v.* hrát
please *interj.* prosím
pleasure *n.* radost
plum *n.* švestka
plural *n. gram.* množné číslo
P.M. *n.* odpoledne
pocket *n.* kapsa
police *n.* policie
police officer *n.* policista
pork *n.* vepřové maso
porridge *n.* ovesná kaše
port *n.* přístav
position *n.* místo
possibility *n.* možnost
post *n.* pošta
postcard *n.* pohlednice
potato *n.* brambor
potential *adj.* možný
poultry *n.* drůbež
powder *n.* prášek
power *n.* síla
praise *n.* chvála

preach *v.* kázat
preface *n.* předmluva
prefer *v.* dávat přednost
preparation *n.* příprava
prepare *v.* připravit
preposition *n. gram.* předložka
prescription *n.* recept
presence *n.* účast
present *adj.* přítomný
present *n.* dárek
present *v.* předvést
press *n.* tisk
pressure *n.* tlak
pretty *adj.* hezký
prevent *v.* zabránit
previously *adv.* předtím
price *n.* cena
primary *adj.* základní
prime *adj.* první
principal *n.* rektor
prior *adj.* dřívější
priority *n.* přednost
prison *n.* věznice
prize *n.* cena
probably *adv.* pravděpodobný
proceeding *n.* postup
processing *n.* zpracování
product *n.* výrobek
profession *n.* povolání
profit *n.* zisk
progress *n.* pokrok
project *n.* plán
promise *v.* slíbit
promote *v.* povýšit
pronoun *n. gram.* zájmeno
proper *adj.* vlastní
proposal *n.* návrh

protect *v.* chránit
protection *n.* ochrana
proud *adj.* hrdý
prove *v.* dokázat
provide *v.* opatřit
provisions *n. pl.* potraviny
pub *n.* hospoda
public *adj.* veřejný
publication *n.* vydání
publish *v.* vydat
pull *v.* /za/táhnout
pumpkin *n.* tykev
pursue *v.* pronásledovat
push *v.* tlačit
put *v.* dát

Q

quality *n.* kvalita
quantity *n.* množství
quarrel *n.* hádka
quarter *n.* čtvrt
queen *n.* královna
question *n.* otázka
question *v.* ptát se
quick *adj.* rychlý
quickly *adv.* rychle
quiet *adj.* tichý
quite *adv.* dost
quote *v.* citovat

R

rabbit *n.* králík
race *n.* běh

railroad *n.* železnice
rain *n.* déšť
raise *v.* /po/zvednout
raisin *n.* hrozinka
range *n.* řada
rapidly *adv.* rychle
rare *adj.* řídký
rather *adv.* poněkud
raw *adj.* syrový
reach *v.* sahat
read *v.* číst
ready *adj.* připravený
real *adj.* skutečný
realize *v.* uvědomit si
reason *n.* důvod
reasonable *adj.* rozumný
receipt *n.* stvrzenka
receive *v.* dostat
recently *adv.* nedávno
recognize *v.* poznat
recommend *v.* doporučit
record *n.* záznam
recover *v.* zotavit se
red *adj.* červený
reduce *v.* zmenšit
reference *n.* poznámka
refreshment *n.* občerstvení
refrigerator *n.* lednička
refuse *v.* odmitnout
regard *v.* považovat
region *n.* oblast
register *v.* záznamenat
regular *adj.* pravidelný
reject *v.* odmítnout
relationship *n.* vztah
religion *n.* náboženství
remember *v.* vzpomenout si

rent *n.* nájemné
repair *n.* oprava
repeat *v.* opakovat
reply *v.* odpovědět
report *n.* zpráva
republic *n.* republika
require *v.* vyžadovat
research *n.* výzkum
resident *n.* místní občan
respect *n.* úcta
respond *v.* odpovídat
response *n.* odpověď
rest *n.* odpočinek
restaurant *n.* restourace
return *n.* návrat
revolution *n.* revoluce
rice *n.* rýže
right *adv.* napravo
ring *n.* prsten
river *n.* řeka
road *n.* silnice
roof *n.* střecha
room *n.* pokoj
root *n.* kořen
route *n.* cesta
royal *adj.* královský
rule *n.* pravidlo
run *n.* běh
rural *adj.* venkovský

S

sack *n.* pytel
safe *adj.* bezpečný
sale *n.* prodej
salt *n.* sůl

same *adj.* stejný
Saturday *n.* sobota
sauce *n.* omáčka
save *v.* zachránit
say *v.* říci
scale *n.* měřítko
scene *n.* scéna
school *n.* škola
science *n.* věda
scissors *n. pl.* nůžky
sea *n.* moře
search *v.* hledat
season *n.* roční doba
seat *n.* židle
second *adj.* druhý
secretary *n.* sekretář
security *n.* bezpečnost
see *v.* vidět
seek *v.* hledat
seem *v.* zdát se
sell *v.* prodávat
send *v.* poslat
separate *adj.* oddělený
September *n.* září
series *n.* řada
serious *adj.* vážný
servant *n.* sluha
service *n.* služba
settle *v.* usadit se
seven *num.* sedm
several *num.* několik
shadow *n.* stín
share *n.* díl
she *pron.* ona
shift *v.* přesunout
ship *n.* loď
shoe *n.* bota

shop *n.* obchod
shopping *n.* nakupování
short *adj.* krátký
shoulder *n.* rameno
shout *v.* pokřikovat
show *v.* ukazovat
shut *v.* zavřít
sick *adj.* nemocný
side *n.* strana
similarly *adv.* podobně
simple *adj.* jednoduchý
sing *v.* zpívat
singer *n.* zpěvák
single *adj.* jeden
sink *n.* umývadlo
sir *n.* pán
sister *n.* sestra
sit *v.* sedět
six *num.* šest
size *n.* velikost
skill *n.* znalost
skin *n.* pleť
sky *n.* obloha
sleep *v.* spát
slow *adj.* pomalý
small *adj.* malý
smallest *adj.* nejmenší
smell *v.* vonět
smile *n.* úsměv
smoke *v.* kouřit
so *adv.* tak
soap *n.* mýdlo
soccer *n.* fotbal
social *adj.* společenský
soft *adj.* měkký
soil *n.* půda
soldier *n.* voják

solution *n.* /vy/řešení
some *adj.* nějaký
son *n.* syn
song *n.* píseň
soon *adv.* brzy
sorry *interj.* pardon
sort *n.* druh
soup *n.* polévka
south *n.* jih
space *n.* místo
speak *v.* říci
specific *adj.* určitý
speech *n.* jazyk
spend *v.* utrácet
spice *n.* koření
spinach *n.* špenát
spoon *n.* lžíce
spot *n.* skvrna
spring *n.* jaro
square *n.* náměstí
stand *v.* stát
standard *n.* úroveň
star *n.* hvězda
start *v.* začít
state *n.* stát
statement *n.* formulace
station *n.* stanice
stay *v.* zůstat
step *n.* krok
stick *v.* /za/píchnout
still *adv.* dosud
stop *n.* zastávka
stop *v.* zastavit
store *n.* obchod
story *n.* příběh
street *n.* ulice
streetcar *n.* tramvaj

strong *adj.* pevný
study *v.* studovat
subject *n.* předmět
subway *n.* metro
succeed *v.* mít úspěch
success *n.* úspěch
successful *adj.* úspěšný
such *adj.* takový
sugar *n.* cukr
suit *n.* oblek
suitable *adj.* vhodný
suitcase *n.* kufr
summer *n.* léto
sun *n.* slunce
Sunday *n.* neděle
sunrise *n.* svítání
sunset *n.* západ slunce
supermarket *n.* samoobsluha
supper *n.* večeře
suppose *v.* předpokládat
sure *adj.* jistý
surname *n.* přímení
surprise *n.* překvapení
sweater *n.* svetr
sweet *adj.* sladký
swim *v.* plavat
swimming pool *n.* bazén
switch *n.* vypínač
syrup *n.* sirup

T

table *n.* stůl
take *v.* vzít
talented *adj.* nadaný
talk *n.* rozhovor
talk *v.* mluvit

tall *adj.* vysoký
tape *n.* páska
taste *n.* chuť
taste *v.* ochutnat
tax *n.* poplatek
tea *n.* čaj
teach *v.* učit
teacher *n.* učitel
tear *n.* roztrhnutí
tear (from eye) *n.* slza
tell *v.* říci
temperature *n.* teplota
ten *num.* deset
term *n.* doba
texture *n.* tkanina
thank *v.* děkovat
thanks *n.* dík
theater *n.* divadlo
them *pron.* jich, jim
then *adv.* pak
there *adv.* tam
they *pron.* oni, ony
thick *adj.* silný
thin *adj.* tenký
thing *n.* věc
think *v.* myslet
thirst *n.* žízeň
thought *n.* myšlenka
thread *n.* nit
three *adj.* tři
throat *n.* krk
through *prep.* přes
throughout *prep.* po
throw *v.* hodit
Thursday *n.* čtvrtek
ticket *n.* lístek
ticket office *n.* pokladna

time *n.* čas
tip *n.* spropitné
tire *n.* pneumatika
tired *adj.* unavený
toast *n.* topinka
tobacco *n.* tabák
today *adv.* dnes
toe *n.* prst na noze
together *adv.* dohromady
toilet *n.* záchod, toaleta
toilet paper *n.* toaletní papír
tomato *n.* rajče
tomorrow *adv.* zítra
tongue *n.* jazyk
tooth *n.* zub
toothbrush *n.* kartáček na zuby
toothpaste *n.* pasta na zuby
total *adj.* celkový
touch *n.* dotek
touch *v.* doktnout se
tour *n.* cesta
towards *prep.* k
towel *n.* ručník
tower *n.* věž
town *n.* město
toy *n.* hračka
trade *n.* obhod
tradition *n.* tradice
traffic *n.* doprava
train *n.* vlak
tram *n.* tramvaj
transport *n.* doprava
travel *n.* cestování
travel *v.* cestovat
treat *v.* ošetřovat
treatment *n.* léčba
tree *n.* strom

trend *n.* móda
trip *n.* cesta
trouble *n.* problém
trousers *n. pl.* kalhoty
true *adj.* pravdivý
trust *n.* víra
trust *v.* důvěřovat
truth *n.* pravda
try *v.* zkusit
Tuesday *n.* úterý
turn *n.* otočení
turn *v.* otočit
twice *adv.* dvakrát
two *num.* dva

U

ugly *adj.* ošklivý
umbrella *n.* deštník
unable *adj.* neschopný
under *prep.* pod
understand *v.* rozumět
unemployment *n.* nezaměstnanost
unfortunately *adv.* naneštěstí
union *n.* spojení
unite *v.* sjednotit
university *n.* univerzita
unknown *adj.* neznámý
unlock *v.* odemknout
until *prep.* až
unusual *adj.* nezvyklý
up *adv.* nahoře
upper *adj.* horní
urban *adj.* městský
urgent *adj.* naléhavý

urine *n.* moč
use *v.* užít
useful *adj.* užitečný
usual *adj.* obvyklý

V

vacation *n.* dovolená
vaccination *n.* očkování
value *n.* hodnota
variation *n.* změna
variety *n.* varieté
vase *n.* váza
vast *adj.* ohromný
veal *n.* telecí maso
vegetable *n.* zelenina
vehicle *n.* vůz
vein *n.* žíla
venison *n.* zvěřina
verb *n. gram.* sloveso
vertebra *n.* obratel
vertigo *n.* závrať
very *adv.* velmi
via *prep.* přes
victory *n.* vítězství
view *n.* výhled
view *v.* prohlížet si
village *n.* vesnice
vinegar *n.* ocet
vision *n.* zrak
visit *n.* návštěva
visit *v.* navštívit
vital *adj.* nezbytný
voice *n.* hlas
vomit *v.* zvracet
vote *n.* hlasování
vote *v.* volit

W

wage *n.* mzda
waist *n.* pas
wait *v.* čekat
waiter *n.* číšník
wake up *v.* vzbudit /se/
walk *v.* jít
wall *n.* stěna
wallet *n.* peněženka
walnut *n.* vlašský ořech
want *v.* chtít
war *n.* válka
warm *adj.* teplý
warn *v.* varovat
wary *adj.* opatrný
wash *v.* prát
washing machine *n.* pračka
wasp *n.* vosa
watch *n.* hodinky
watch *v.* dívat se
water *n.* voda
wave (on the water) *n.* vlna (na vodě)
way *n.* cesta
we *pron.* my
weak *adj.* slabý
wear *v.* nosit
weather *n.* počasí
Wednesday *n.* středa
week *n.* týden
weekend *n.* víkend
weigh *v.* vážit
weight *n.* váha
welcome *v.* vítat
well *adv.* dobře
west *n.* západ

wet *adj.* mokrý
what *pron.* co, kolik
when *adv.* kdy
where *adv.* kde, kam
which *pron.* který
while *n.* chvíle
white *adj.* bílý
who *pron.* kdo
whole *adj.* celý
why *adv.* proč
wide *adj.* široký
wife *n.* manželka
win *v.* zvítězit
wind *n.* vítr
window *n.* okno
wine *n.* víno
winter *n.* zima
wish *v.* přát si
with *prep.* s
without *prep.* bez
woman *n.* žena
wonderful *adj.* báječný
wood *n.* les
wool *n.* vlna
word *n.* slovo
work *n.* práce
work *v.* pracovat
worker *n.* pracovník
world *n.* svět
wound *n.* rána
wrap *v.* zabalit
wrapper *n.* obálka
write *v.* psát
writer *n.* spisovatel
writing *n.* písmo
wrong *adj.* nesprávný

X

X-ray *n.* rentgenový paprsek

Y

yard *n.* dvůr
year *n.* rok
yellow *adj.* žlutý
yes *adv.* ano
yesterday *adv.* včera
yet *adv.* už
yolk *n.* žloutek
you *pron.* ty; vy
young *adj.* mladý
your *adj.* tvůj; váš; svůj (tvoje; vaše; vaši)
yours *pron.* tvůj; váš
youth *n.* mládí

Z

zero *n.* nula
zodiac *n.* zvěrokruh
zoo *n.* zoologická zahrada

CZECH PHRASEBOOK

TABLE OF CONTENTS

1. ETIQUETTE AND BASICS

Greetings and Goodbyes

Good morning.
Dobré ráno.

Good afternoon.
Dobré odpoledne.

Good evening.
Dobrý večer.

Hi; Hello.
Ahoj.

See you; Goodbye.
Na shledanou.

Bye.
Ahoj.

Good night.
Dobrou noc.

Polite Expressions

How are you?
Jak se máte? Jak se vám daří?

I am fine, thanks. And you?
Děkuji, dobře. A vy?

Please
Prosím

Many thanks.
Děkuji moc. Mockrát vám děkuji.

You are welcome.
Za nic. Za málo.

Excuse me!
Promiňte!

I apologize.
Omlouvám se.

Sorry.
Promiňte, s dovdlením.

It does not matter.
Nic se nestalo.

All right.
Dobře.

Congratulations

Congratulations.
Blahopřeji.

Happy birthday.
Vše nejlepší k narozeninám.

Merry Christmas and Happy New Year.
Veselé Vánoce a šťastný Nový rok.

Happy Easter.
Veselé Velikonoce.

I wish you a lot of success.
Přeji Vám mnoho úspěchů.

Useful Expressions

Is that so?	**Je to tak?**
I want …	**Chtěl/a bych …**
I do not want …	**Nechci …**
Where is …	**Kde je …**
When does it open? …close?	**Kdy je otevřeno? …zavřeno?**
I am looking for …	**Hledám …**

Can you recommend a …
Můžete mi doporučit …
Můžete mi poradit …

Can you help me, please?
Můžete mi pomoc, prosím?

Good.	**Dobře.**
It is bad.	**To je špatně.**
It's my fault.	**Je to moje chyba.**
It's not my fault.	**Není to moje chyba.**
I know.	**Vím.**
I don't know.	**Nevím.**
Wait a minute.	**Vyčkejte chvilku.**
	Počkejte chvilku.

Come in.	**Vstupte.**
Come here.	**Přiďte jsem.**
Go there.	**Jeťte tam.**
Stop here.	**Zastavte tady.**
Here.	**Tady.**
There.	**Tam.**
Welcome.	**Srdečně vás vítáme.**
Can I help you?	**Mohu vám pomoci?**
What time is it?	**Kolik je hodin?**
What is wrong?	**Co je nesprávné?**
Listen.	**Poslouchat.**
Be careful!	**Opatrně!**
Come quickly.	**Přiď rychle.**
	Přiďte rychle.
I am hungry.	**Mám hlad.**
I am thirsty.	**Mám žízeň.**
I am not hungry.	**Nemám hlad.**
I am not thirsty.	**Nemám žízeň.**
I am sorry.	**Promiňte.**
I am tired.	**Jsem unavený/á.**
I am sad.	**Jsem smutný/á.**
I am full.	**Stačí mi to.**
I am cold.	**Nachladil/a jsem se.**
I am hot.	**Je mi horko.**

Questions

Who?	**Kdo?**
Why?	**Proč?**
When?	**Kdy?**
Where?	**Kde?**
What?	**Co?**
How?	**Jak?**
What is that?	**Co je to?**
What is this?	**Co je toto?**
Who is that?	**Kdo je to?**

2. LANGUAGE

Do you speak English?
Mluvíte anglicky?

Yes, I do.
Ano, mluvím.

Just a bit.
Trochu.

I don't speak English.
Nemluvím anglicky.

I don't speak Czech.
Neumím česky.

I speak a little Czech.
Umím trošku česky.

I don't understand.
Nerozumím.

Could you speak more slowly?
Mohl/a byste mluvit pomaleji?

Could you repeat it, please?
Mohl/a byste to zopakovat, prosím?

Could you write that down, please?
Mohl/a byste to napsat, prosím?

What does that mean?
Co to znamena?

How do you say … in English?
Jak se řekne anglicky … ?

How do you say … in Czech?
Jak se řekne česky … ?

How do you spell it?
Jak se to hláskuje?

How do you pronounce this?
Jak se to vyslovuje?

3. INTRODUCTIONS

Let me introduce myself.
Dovolte, abych se přestavil/a.

My name is …
Jmenuji se …

Nice to meet you.
Těší mě.

Do you know Mr./Mrs./Miss …
Znáte pána/paní/slečnu …

What is your name?
Jak se jmenujte? Jaké je vaše jméno?

I am from …	**(Já) jsem z …**
America	**Ameriky**
England	**Anglije**
Canada	**Kanady**
Australia	**Austálie**

I am …	**(Já) jsem …**
American	**Američan**
English	**Angličan**
Canadian	**Kanaďan**
Australian	**Australan**

Other Nationalities:

Albania / Albanian	**Albansko / Albánec**
Austria/Austrian	**Rakousko / Rakušan**
Bulgaria/Bulgarian	**Bulharsko / Bulhar**
Croatia / Croat	**Chorvatsko / Chorvat**
Europe / European	**Evropa / Evropan**

France / French	**Francie / Francouz**
Germany / German	**Německo / Němec**
Great Britain /British	**Velká Britanie / Brit**
(English, Scottish, Welsh)	**(Angličan, Skot, Velšan)**
Greece / Greek	**Řecko / Řek**
Holland / Dutch	**Holandsko, Nizozemí /**
	Holaňd'an, Nizozemec
Hungary /Hungarian	**Maďarsko / Maďar**
Italy / Italian	**Italsko / Ital**
Ireland / Irish	**Irsko / Ir**
Poland / Polish	**Polsko / Polák**
Portugal /Portuguese	**Portugalsko /**
	Portugalec
Romania / Romanian	**Rumunsko / Rumun**
Russia / Russian	**Rusko / Rus**
Serbia / Serb	**Srbsko / Srb**
Slovakia / Slovak	**Slovensko / Slovák**
Switzerland / Swiss	**Švýcarsko / Švýcar**
I speak …	**Umím … Mluvím …**
English	**anglicky**
Czech	**česky**
Dutch	**holandsky**
French	**francouzky**
German	**německy**
Italian	**italsky**
Polish	**polsky**
Portuguese	**portugalsky**
Russian	**rusky**
Spanish	**španělsky**
Slovak	**slovensky**

I do not speak Czech.
Nemluvím česky. Neumím česky.

I speak a little Czech.
Umím trochu česky. Mluvím trochu česky.

Do you speak English?
Mluvíte anglicky?

I am a …	(Já) jsem …
student	**student**
doctor	**lékař**
businessperson	**obchodník**
lawyer	**právník, advokát**
journalist	**žurnalista**
engineer	**inženýr**
salesperson	**prodavač**
waiter/waitress	**číšník / servírka**
librarian	**knihovník**
computer programmer	**programátor na počítače**
teacher	**učitel**
secretary	**sekretář**
travel agent	**cestovní jednatel**
musician	**hudebník, muzikant**
scientist	**vědec**
police officer	**policista**
soldier	**voják**

I study …	Já studuji … Studuji …
art	**umění**
biology	**biologii**
business	**ekonomiku**
history	**dějiny**
law	**právo**
literature	**literaturu**
medicine	**medicínu**
music	**hudbu**
psychology	**psychologii**
theater	**divadelné umění**

This is my …	**To je …**
mother	**moje matka**
father	**můj otec**
sister	**moje sestra**
brother	**můj bratr**
son	**můj syn**
daughter	**moje dcera**
husband	**můj mažel**
wife	**moje manželka**
grandmother	**moje babička**
grandfather	**můj dědeček**
uncle	**můj strýc**
aunt	**moje teta**
cousin	**můj bratranec;**
	moje sestřenice
friend	**můj kamarád**

Do you have children? **Máte děti?**

Are you married? **Jste ženatý?**
Jste provdaná?

I am married. **Jsem ženatý.**
Jsem provdaná.

I am single. **Jsem svobodný/**
neženatý.

We are on vacation.
Tady jsme na dovolené.

I am here to study.
Zde studuji.

4. TRAVEL AND TRANSPORTATION

May I ask you?
Mohu se zeptat?

Where are we?
Kde to jsme?

Which bus /streetcar goes to the town center?
Který autobus/která tramvaj jede do střed města?

Take a number 6 bus.
Jeďte autobusem číslo 6. / Vemte autobus čislo 6.

I want to go to ...	**Chtěl/a bych jít do ...**
...town.	**...města.**
...the store.	**...obchodního domu.**

Where can I buy a ticket to...?
Kde se prodávají jízdenky do...?

one-way ticket	**jednosměrná jízdenka**
round trip ticket	**okružní jízdní jízdenka**

Where can I find a travel agency?
Kde bych mohl/a najít cestovní kancelář?

Where is the ...?	**Kde je ...?**
...bus station	**...stanice autobusu; zastávka autobusu**
...train station	**...nádraží**
...streetcar station	**...stanice tramvaje**
...subway station	**...stanice metra**
...subway	**...metro**

What is the name of this street?
Jak se jmenuje tato ulice?

Show me on the map, please.
Ukažte mi to na mapě, prosím.

Customs

Customs examination
Celní kontrola

Please show your passport/visa.
Prosím, ukažte mi, váš pas/vízum.

Here is my passport/visa.
Prosím, tady máte, můj pas/vízum.

I am on vacation.
Jsem na dovolené.

I am a student.
Jsem student.

I will stay for two/four days/weeks/months.
Zůstanu dva/čtyři dny/týdny/měsíce.

Do you have anything to declare?
Máte něco k proclení?

I've got nothing to declare.
Nemám nic k proclení.

Open your bag, please.
Otevřete, prosím vaši tašku.

These are gifts.
To jsou dárky.

I'd like to declare this.
Chtěl/a bych toto proclít.

Whose suitcase is this?
Čí je ten kufr?

What do you have in the bag?
Co máte v té tašce?

Here is my luggage.
Tady jsou moje zavazadla.

Shall I open it?
Mám je otevřít?

May I close it?
Mohu je zavřít?

Here is my passport.
Tady je můj pas.

This is all I have.
To je vše co mám.

All these are my clothes.
To vše je moje šatstvo/oblečení.

This suitcase contains only books.
Toto zavazadlo obsahuje jenom knihy.

Must I pay a duty?
Musím zaplatit clo?

Travel by Plane

Which bus goes to the airport?
Který autobus jede na letiště?

Where is the airport?
Kde je letiště?

How far is it?
Jak je to daleko?

Can you book me for Monday?
Můžete mi udělat rezervaci na pondělí?

I would like a first-class seat.
Chtěl/a bych místo v první třídě.

Your flight has been delayed.
Váš let byl zrušen.

That flight is full.
Letadlo je plně obsazeno.

I have lost my bag. Please help me.
Stratil/a jse mi taška. Prosím, pomozte mi.

I have lost my ticket.
Stratil/a jsem letenku.

I have missed my flight.
Zmeškal/a jsem svůj let.

I would like ...	**Chtěl/a bych ...**
...something to drink	**...něco k pití**
...something to eat	**...něco k jídlu**
...some coffee	**...trochu kávy**

...tea	**...čaj**
...a newspaper	**...noviny**
...a magazine	**...časopis**
...some water	**...vodu**

airplane	**letadlo**
airport	**letiště**
arrival	**příjezd, přílet**
departure	**odjezd, odlet**
boarding pass	**palubní vstupenka**
entrance	**vchod**
exit	**východ**
flight	**let**
gate	**vchod; východ**
no entry	**vstup zakázán**
no smoking	**kouření zakázáno**

Travel by Bus and Streetcar

Where can I get a bus schedule/streetcar schedule?
Kde můžu dostat plán autobusů/ tramvaji?

Where can I get a bus/streetcar map?
Kde můžu dostat mapu autobusů/tramvaji?
**Kde můžu dostat mapu autobusů/elektrických
    drah?**

Where is the nearest bus station/streetcar station?
**Kde je nejbližší stanice autobusu/stanice
    tramvaje?**

Where does the bus/the streetcar stop?
Kde staví autobus/tramvaj?

Does this bus/streetcar go to the theater?
Jede tento autobus/tato tramvaj k divadlu?

When is the next bus/streetcar?
Kdy je další autobus/tramvaj?

Where can I buy a ticket?
Kde si můžu koupit lístek?

How much is the ticket?
Kolik stojí jeden lístek?

driver	**řidič**
fare	**jízdné**
number	**číslo**
schedule	**plan, rozpis, jízdní řád**
station	**stanice**
stop	**zastávka**
transfer	**přesednout, přestoupit**
ticket	**lístek; jízdenka**

Travel by Subway

subway station	**stanice metra**
token	**znamení, znak**
emergency brake	**nouzová brzda**
subway map	**mapa metra**
subway stop	**zastávka metra**
conductor	**průvodčí**
fine, penalty	**pokuta**

Attention, the door is closing.
Pozor, dveře se zavírají.

Attention, the door is opening.
Pozor, dveře se otevírají.

Travel by Train

Which train goes to …?
Který vlak jede do …?

From which platform?
Které nástupiště?

At what time?
V kolik hodin?

Taxi

Where can I get a taxi?
Kde najdu taxi?

Please stop here.
Prosím, zastavte tady.

Can you wait here, please?
Můžete tady počkat, prosím?

Are you free?
Jste volný?

Call a taxi for me, please?
Zavolejte mi taxi, prosím?

How much does it cost?
Kolik to stojí?

Would you take me ...?	**Ovdezl/a byste mne ...?**
...downtown	**...do centra města**
...to the hotel	**...do hotelu**
...to the airport	**...na letiště**
...to the train station	**...na nádraží**

bicycle	**kolo**
bus stop	**autobusová zastávka**
car	**auto**
road	**silnice**
station	**zastávka**
train	**vlak**
train station	**nádraží**

The Car

In the Czech Republic, kilometers are used in place of miles (1 mile = 1.6 kilometers).

Foreigners should have an international driver's license. Speed limits are 50 kilometers per hour in towns, 80 km/h on main roads and 120 km/h on highways. First class roads are in good condition and roadside assistance is available. To drive legally on major highways, a tax sticker is required (available at gasoline stations). Highway signs are green, while main road and city signs are blue. Yellow fields mean no parking and blue fields mean limited parking with visible parking permit behind the windshield. Seat belts are required. Special attention is required when driving among streetcars in historic city centers.

I have an international driver's license.
Mám mezinárodní řidičský průkaz.

Where can I rent ...?	**Kde muhu pronajmout ...?**
...a car	**...auto**
...a motorcycle	**...motorku**
...a bicycle	**...kolo**

How much is it per day?	**Kolik to stojí na den?**
...per week?	**...na týden?**
...for two days?	**...na dva dny?**
...for five days?	**...na pět dnů?**

Where is the nearest gas station?
Kde je nejbližší benzinová stanice?

Fill it up, please.
Prosím, plnou nádrž.

Check the ..., please.	**Zkontrolujte, prosím, ...**
battery	**baterii**
brake fluid	**brzdovou tekutinu**
oil/water	**olej/vodu**

driver's license	**řidičský průkaz**
insurance policy	**pojišťovna**
car paper	**autodoklady**
front seat	**přední místo**
back seat	**zadní místo**

Asking for Directions

Where is the ...?	**Kde je ...?**
...airport	**...letiště**
...art gallery	**...umělecká galérie**

...bank	**...banka**
...church	**...kostel**
...downtown	**...centrum/**
	střed města
...market	**...tržnice**
...station	**...zastávka**

Can you show me the route on the map?
Můžete mi ukázat cestu na mapě?

How many kilometers is it to Prague?
Kolik je to kilometrů do Prahy?

Is there a highway?
Je tam dálnice?

What's the name of this street?
Jak se jmenuje tato ulice?

Where can I find this address?
Kde mohu najít tuto adresu?

It is near.	**Je blízko.**
Is it near?	**Je to blízko?**

It is far.	**Je daleko.**
Is it far?	**Je to daleko?**
How far is it?	**Jak je to daleko?**

Can I park here?
Mohu zde zaparkovat?

How do I get to ...?
Jak se dostanu k ...?

I want to get to ...
Chci se dostat na ...

Turn left.	**Zatočte doleva.**
Turn right.	**Zatočte doprava.**

behind	**za, vzadu**
corner	**roh**
far	**daleko**
near	**blízko**
right	**doprava**
left	**doleva**

north	**sever**
south	**jih**
east	**východ**
west	**západ**

parking	**parkoviště**
stop	**zastavit**

5. MONEY

The official currency in the Czech Republic is the Czech crown (**koruna**), divided into one hundred hellers (**haléř**).

Where is the nearest bank?
Kde je nejbližší banka?

Where can I change money?
Kde se dají vyměnit peníze?

What is the exchange rate?
Jaký je kurs?

What's the present rate of exchange for the US
 dollar to the Czech crown?
**Jaký je dnešní kurs amerického dolaru k české
 koruně?**

I want to open a savings account.
Chtěl/a bych otevřít spožitelní účet.

borrow	**půjčit**
cash	**hotové peníze**
change	**vyměna**
coins	**mince, drobné**
exchange	**směnárna**
money	**peníze**
return	**vrátit**
signature	**podpis**

6. COMMUNICATIONS

Where can I phone from?
Odkud se dá telefonovat?

Where is the nearest public phone?
Kde je nejbližší telefonní budka?

Where is the telephone?
Kde je telefon?

May I telephone from here?
Mohu si odtud zatelefonovat?

I want to make a local call.
Chci provést místní hovor.

I want to make an international call.
Chci provést mezinárodní hovor.

Do you have a telephone directory?
Máte telefonní seznam?

My number is ...
Moje telefonní číslo je ...

How much does it cost?
Kolik to stojí?

It is ... crowns.
Je to ... korun. Stojí to ... korun.

Hello
Haló

This is Karel speaking.
U telefonu je Karel.

Can I leave a message?
Mohu nechat vzkaz?

I will call again.
Zavolám znovu.

Ask him to call this number.
Popros ho, vytočit toto telefonní číslo.

There is a call for you.
Někdo Vás volal.

Fax

I wish to send a fax.
Chci poslat fax.

Can I send/receive faxes here?
Mohl/a bych poslat/dostat fax tady?

What is your fax number?
Jaké je vaše číslo faxu?

How much is it per page?
Kolik stojí jedna stránka?

Post Office

Where is the nearest post office?
Kde je nejbližší pošta?

Where is the main post office?
Kde je hlavní pošta?

I would like to send ...	**Chtěl/a bych poslat ...**
...a postcard	**...pohlednici**
...a parcel	**...balíček**
...a telegram	**...telegram**

I would like to send this letter ...	**Chtěl/a bych poslat tento dopis ...**
...by registered mail	**...doporučeně**
...express delivery	**...expres**
...by airmail	**...letecky**

I am looking for a mailbox.
Hledám poštovní schránku.

I want to buy stamps.
Chci koupit známky.

How many stamps do I need?
Kolik známek je zapotřebí?

Give me ..., please.	**Dejte mi ..., prosím.**
...one stamp	**...jedu známku**
...two stamps	**...dvě známky**
...five stamps	**...pět známek**

Internet Services

I am looking for the Internet.
Hledám Internet.

Is there an Internet cafe in town?
Je ve městě Internet cafe?

I want to send an e-mail to my friend.
Chtěl/a bych poslat e-mail svému kamarádovi.

How much does it cost to use the Internet?
Kolik stojí použití Internetu?

computer	**počítač**
e-mail	**e-mail**
enter	**zapsat**
letter	**dopis**
number	**číslo**
password	**heslo**

7. ACCOMMODATIONS

I am looking for a furnished apartment.
Hledám zařízený byt.

I am looking for an unfurnished apartment.
Hledám nezařízený byt.

How much is it per month?
Kolik to stojí měsíčně?

Where do I pay for water and electricity?
Kde se platí za vodu a elektřinu?

Hotel

I am looking for a good hotel.	**Hledám dobrý hotel.**
...an inexpensive hotel.	**...levný hotel.**

How much is it per room?
Kolik stojí jeden pokoj?

Is breakfast included?
Je v ceně snídaně?

I would like ...	**Chtěl/a bych ...**
...a single room	**...jednolužkový pokoj**
...a double room	**...dvoulužkový pokoj**
We would like ...	**Chěli bychom ...**
...a room	**...pokoj**
...two rooms	**...dva pokoje**

Accommodations

It costs … per night.	**Stojí to … na noc.**
I want a room with …	**Chci pokoj …**
…a bathroom	**…s koupelnou**
…a shower	**…se sprchou**
…a television	**…s televizí**
…a telephone	**…s telefonem**
I will stay for …	**Zůstanu …**
…one day	**…jeden den**
…two days	**…dva dny**
…five days	**…pět dnů**

My name is …
Jmenuji se …

I would like to get my bill.
Chtěl/a bych dostat účet.

Can I pay with a check?	**Mohu platit šekem?**
…a credit card?	**…kreditní kartou?**

Please bring me …	**Prosím, přineste mi …**
…a towel	**…ručník**
…a glass	**…sklenici**
…soap	**…mýdlo**
…a pillow	**…polštář**

Please bring me some …	**Přineste mi, prosím trochu …**
…water	**…vody**
…juice	**…štávy**

Can I wash these clothes?
Mohu si vyprat tyto věci?

I am in room 9.
Jsem v pokoji č. (číslo) 9 (devět).

bathroom	**koupelna**
bed	**postel**
bill	**účet**
blanket	**deka**
cloth	**utěrka**
double bed	**dvojlůžko**
electricity	**elektřina**
ice	**led**
key	**klíč**
mattress	**matrace**
mirror	**zrcadlo**
name	**jméno**
pillow	**polštář**
refrigerator	**lednička**
restroom	**toaleta, WC**
room	**pokoj**
shower	**sprcha**
suitcase	**zavazadlo**
water	**voda**
cold water	**studená voda**
warm water	**teplá voda**
hot water	**vřelá, horká voda**

8. FOOD AND DRINK

The Czech national dish is pork, cabbage, and dumplings.

Breakfast
Snídaně

Lunch
Oběd

Dinner
Večeře

Salad
Salát

Starter/appetizer
Předkrm

Main course
Hlavní jídla

Dessert
Zákusek

I am full.
Najet jsem se. Stačí mi to.

I am hungry.
Mám hlad.

I am thirsty.
Mám žízeň.

Waiter!/Waitress!
Pane číšníku!/Paní servírko!

I would like to make a reservation.
Chtěl/a bych udělat rezervaci.
Chtěl/a bych rezervovat.

A table for two, please.
Stůl pro dva, prosím.

Is this table free?
Je tento stůl volný?

Are these seats free?
Jsou tu volná místa?

The menu, please.
Jídelní lístek, prosím.

Wine list.
Nápojový lístek.

We'd like to order.
Chtěli bychom si objednat.

Can you recommend something?
Můžete něco doporučit?

Do you have a children's menu?
Mate děcká jídla?

I'd like …
Chtěl/a bych …

I am a vegetarian.
Jsem vegetarián.

What would you like to drink?
Co si dáte k pití?

I didn't order this.
Tohle jsem si neobjednal/a.

It was delicious.
Bylo to výborné.

This is overcooked/undercooked.
Je to převařené, přepečené/nedovažené, nedopečené.

This is not hot/cold.
Není to teplé/studené.

Where is the restroom, please?
Kde jsou tady toalety, prosím?

Could I have the bill?
Mohu dostat účet?

The bill, please.
Účet, prosím.

Here is your bill.
Zde je váš účet.

Here is your tip.
Tady máte vaše spropitné.

I think the bill is incorrect.
Myslím, že účet nesouhlasí.

Could you give me...?	**Mohl/a byste mi podat...?**
...sugar	**...cukr**
...bread	**...chléb**
...a knife	**...nůž**

…an ashtray	**…popelník**
…a glass	**…sklenici**
…a cup	**…šálek**

I would like…	**Dal/a bych si…**
…tea	**…čaj**
…coffee	**…kávu**
…milk	**…mléko**
…cocoa	**…kakao**
…juice	**…šťávu**
…water	**…vodu**
…beer	**…pivo**
…dark	**…černé**
…light	**…světlé**
…draught	**…točené**
…lager	**…ležák**
…pilsner	**…plzeňské**
…ice cream	**…zmrzlinu**

napkin	**ubrousek**
fork	**vidlička**
spoon	**polévková lžíce**
salt	**sůl**
pepper	**pepř**

Fruits

apple	**jablko**
apricot	**meruňka**
banana	**banán**
grapes	**hrozny**
lemon	**citron**
peach	**broskev**
plum	**švestka**

Vegetables

cabbage	**hlávkové zelí**
carrot	**mrkev**
cucumber	**okurka**
green beans	**želené fazole**
green peas	**želený hrášek**
lentils	**čočka**
mushroom	**houby, žampiony**
onion	**cibule**
potatoes	**brambory**
spinach	**špenát**
tomato	**rajče, rajské jablko**

Food

beans	**fazole**
beef	**hovězí maso**
chicken	**kuře**
cream	**smetana**
duck	**kachna**
dumpling	**knedlík**
fillet steak	**řízek**
fish	**ryba**
ham	**šunka**
lamb chop	**jehněčí kotlety**
ground meat	**mleté maso**
mutton	**skopové maso**
pork	**vepřové maso**
sausages	**párky; uzeniny**
steak	**biftek**
veal	**telecí maso**

9. SHOPPING

When do the shops open/close?
V kolik hodin otevírají/zavírají obchody?

I want to go shopping.
Potřebuji jít nakoupit.

Where can I buy ...?
Kde se dá koupit ...?

Can you take me to the shopping mall?
Můžete mě zavést do obchodního domu?

I need some things.
Potřebuji několik věcí.

Please, wrap this for me.
Prosím, zabalte mi to.

How much does it cost?
Kolik to stojí?

Where do I pay?
Kde mohu zaplatit?

Stores

Where can I find a ...?   **Kde najdu ...?**
  ...bakery   **...pekárnu**
  ...bookstore   **...knihkupectví**
  ...butcher's   **...řeznictví**
  ...clothing store   **...dům oděvů**
  ...drugstore   **...drogerii**
  ...florist   **...květinářství**

...fruit store	...obchod s ovocem
...grocery	...potraviny
...market	...tržnici
...music store	...obchod s hudebninami
...pharmacy	...lékárnu
...spice shop	...obchod s kořením
...shoemaker	...obuvníka
...supermarket	...samoobsluhu
...tailor	...krejčího
...watchmaker	...hodináře

Clothing

Can I help you?
Co si přejete?

Where can I get ...?
Kde dostanu ...?

May I try this one?
Mohl/a bych to vyzkoušet?

Does it fit me?
Jde mi to? Sedí mi to?

It's too expensive.
Je to moc drahé.

bigger	**větší**
smaller	**menší**
cheaper	**levnější**
more expensive	**dražší**

women's size	**damská velikost**
men's size	**panská velikost**
children's size	**dětská velikost**
I want to buy a	**Chci koupit ... .**
...bag	**...tašku**
...blouse	**...halenku**
...coat	**...kabát**
...dress	**...šaty, oblečení; oděv**
...handkerchief	**...kapesník**
...hat	**...čepici; klobouk**
...nightgown	**...župan**
...pyjamas	**...pyžamo**
...shoes	**...boty**
...skirt	**...sukni**
...socks	**...ponožky**
...suit	**...oblek**

Drugstore

batteries	**baterie**
comb	**hřeben**
condom	**preservativ**
hairbrush	**kartáček na vlasy**
lipstick	**rtěnka**
painkiller	**lék proti bolesti**
powder	**prášek**
razor	**holící strojek**
shampoo	**šampón**
soap	**mýdlo**
tissue	**papírový kapesník**
toothbrush	**zubní kartáček**
toothpaste	**zubní pasta**

Bookstore

Where can I find a bookstore?
Kde tady najdu knihkupectví?

Is there a bookstore nearby?
Je tu nedaleko knihkupectví?

Do you have ...?	**Máte, prosím vás, ...?**
...a map	**...mapu**
...a guide to Prague	**...průvodce Prahy**
...a dictionary	**...slovník**
...a novel	**...román**
...English books	**...angličké knihy**

I want to buy ...	**Chci koupit ...**
...a book	**...knihu**
...a magazine	**...časopis**
...a newspaper	**...noviny**
...a notebook	**...zápisník**
...a pen	**...pero**
...a pencil	**...tužku**

Camera and Photographs

I'd like ... film for this camera.	**Chtěl/a bych ... film do tohoto fotoaparátu.**
...black and white...	**...černo-bílý...**
...color...	**...barevný...**

How much does it cost?
Kolik to stojí?

Could you develop this film?
Můžete mi vyvolat tento film?

When will the film be ready?
Kdy bude film hotový?

I'd like a copy of this print.
Chtěl/a bych kopii toho tisku.

battery	**baterie**
enlargement	**zvětšení, rozšíření**
flash	**blesk**
lens	**objektiv**
print	**tisk, otisk**
take a picture	**udělat fotku, vyfotit**

10. SERVICES

At the Beauty Salon

I would like ...	**Chtěl/a bych ...**
...to have a haircut	**...dát se ostříhat**
...hairspray	**...lak na vlasy**
...a shave	**...holení**
...to wash my hair	**...umýt vlasy**
...a massage	**...masáž**
...to make an appointment for tomorrow	**...vzít si/udělat si čas/hodinu na zítřek**

I want my hair colored.
Chtěl/a bych si vlasy obarvit.

I want my hair curled.
Chtěl/a bych trvalou.

Laundry and Dry Cleaning

Where can I take my clothes to be washed?
Kde si mohu nechat vyprát prádlo?

Is there a dry cleaner nearby?
Je blízko chemická čistírna?

I would like to wash these clothes.
Chtěl/a bych vyprat toto prádlo.

Please, separate light and dark-colored clothing.
Prosím, vyperte odděleně tmavé-barevné prádlo.

Do not wash this dress in ...	**Neperte ty šaty v ...**
...hot water	**...horké vodě**
...cold water	**...studené vodě**
...warm water	**...teplé vodě**
I want to iron ...	**Chci vyžehlit ...**
...this dress	**...ty šaty**
...this shirt	**...tu košili**
clothes	**prádlo; oblečení; šatstvo**
dry cleaner	**chemická čistírna**
iron	**žehlička**
water	**voda**

11. CULTURE AND ENTERTAINMENT

Where can I find the theater?
Kde se nachází divadlo?

Please, can you show me on the map?
Můžete mi to ukázat na mapě, prosím?

I would like to go to the theater.
Chtěl/a bych jít do divadla.

Please, do you have a ticket?
Máte vstupenky, prosím?

I would like to go to ... tonight.	**Chtěl/a bych jít dnes večer ... .**
...the cinema	**...do kina**
...a concert	**...na koncert**

How much are the tickets?
Kolik stojí vstupenka?

At what time does it start?
V kolik hodin začíná?

How long is the performance?
Jak dlouho bude trvat představení.

Please, can you show me to my seat?
Prosím, můžete mi ukázat moje místo?

One ticket for today, please.
Jednu vstupenku na dnešek, prosím.

Two tickets for tonight, please.
Dvě vstupenky na dnešní večerní přestavení, prosím.

Five tickets for tomorrow, please.
Pět vstupenek na zítřek, prosím.

in the front	**vepředu**
in the middle	**uprostřed**
in the back	**vzadu**

What kind of music do you like?
Jakou hudbu máte rád/a?

I like ... .   **Mám rád/a ... .**
  ...classical music   **...klasickou hudbu**
  ...pop music   **...populární hudbu**
  ...chamber music   **...komorní hudbu**

castle	**zámek**
church	**kostel**
cinema	**kino**
city walk	**procházka městem**
comedy	**veselohra**
dance	**tanec**
drama	**činohra**
drums	**bubny**
folk/traditional	**lidový/tradiční**
music	**hudba**
organ	**varhany**
performance	**představení**
piano	**klavír**
play	**hra**
row	**řada**
seat	**místo**
theater	**divadlo**
ticket	**lístek, vstupenka**
trumpet	**trubka**
violin	**housle**

Culture and Entertainment

Library

I am looking for a library.
Hledám knihovnu.

Can you show me, please?
Můžete mi ji ukázat, prosím?

book   **kniha**
library   **knihovna**

Museum

opening hours   **návštěvní doba**
adult tickets   **vstupenka pro dospělé**
children's tickets   **vstupenka pro děti**
senior discount   **slevu pro senior**
student discount   **slevu pro studenty**
children's discount   **slevu pro mládež**
guide   **průvodce**
art   **umění**
cafeteria   **kavárna**
exit   **východ**
entry/entrance   **vchod**
coatroom   **šatna**

Where is the coatroom?
Kde je šatna?

put one's coat in coatroom
dát si kabát do šatny

get one's coat from coatroom
vyzvednout si kabát ze šatny

That's not my coat.
To není můj kabát.

Sightseeing

tour	**prohlídka, cesta**
tour in English	**prohlídka v anglickém jazyce**
square	**náměstí**
main square	**hlavní náměstí**
memorial	**památník**
column	**sloup**
building	**budova**
museum	**muzeum**
gallery	**galérie**
art gallery	**galérie výtvarného umění**
cathedral	**katedrála**
exhibition	**výstava**
fair	**veletrtrh, pouť**

Can we take photographs?
Můžeme vyfotografovat/vyfotit/udělat fotku?

12. SPORTS

What kind of sports do you like?
Jaký druh sportu máte rád/a?

I would like to play	**Chtěl/a bych si zahrát ... .**
...tennis	**...tenis**
...soccer	**...fotbal**
...golf	**...golf**
...basketball	**...košíkovou**

Where is a swimming pool?
Kde je bazén?

ball	**míč**
basketball	**košíková**
chess	**šachy**
clock	**hodiny**
coach	**trenér**
game	**hra**
handball	**házená**
rollerskates	**kolečkové brusle**
run	**běh**
skate	**bruslit**
stadium	**stadión**
swim	**plavat**
team	**tým**
volleyball	**odbíjená**
whistle	**hvízdnutí, písknutí**

I would like to watch a game of ... .
Chtěl/a bych se podívat na ... .
Chtěl/a bych sledovat hru ... .

mountain	**hora**
in the mountains	**v horách**
hill	**kopec**
alpine	**vysokohorský**
mountaineer	**horolezec**
mountaineering	**horolezectví**
marked footpath	**turistická cesta**
tourist	**turistický**
hike	**pěší výlet**
hiking tour	**pěší túra**
ski	**lyže**
skiing	**lyžovat**
ski lift	**lyžařský vlek**
sled	**sáňkovat**
go sledding	**jít sáňkovat**
boat, ship	**loď**
travel by boat	**jet na lodí**
sailor	**lodník**
river	**řeka**
down the river	**po řece**

13. HEALTH

Medical facilities are available throughout the Czech Republic. Doctors and hospitals often expect cash payment for health services. Tourists are advised to have medical insurance that is valid worldwide.

I need to see a physician.
Potřebuji lékaře.

Is there a doctor who speaks English?
Je tu lékař, který mluví/umí anglicky?

What is the problem?
Jaké obtíže máte?

I am sick.
Jsem nemocný/á.

My friend is sick.
Můj kamarád je nemocný (M).
Má kamarádka je nemocná (F).

I'd like to make an appointment with a doctor.
Chtěl/a bych sjednat návštěvu u lekáře.

I have health insurance.
Mám zdravotní pojištění.

Where is the nearest hospital?
Kde je nejbližší nemocnice?

Please, call an anbulance.
Prosím, zavolejte sanitku.

bandage	**obvaz**
burn	**spálenina**
emergency room	**reanimace**
medicine	**lék**
painkiller	**lék proti bolesti**
pharmacy	**lékárna**
prescription	**recept, předpis**
surgeon	**chirurg**
mild	**mírný**
serious	**vážný, seriózní**
severe	**oddělit**

Emergency Numbers

Police	158
Municipal police	156
Fire	150
Emergency, First aid	155
Emergency health, children, adult	141-23
Medical emergency service	141-24

Illness

How long have you been sick?
Jak dlouho jste nemocný/a?

Where does it hurt?
Kde vás bolí?

It hurts here.
Tady to bolí.

I have been throwing up.
Zvracel/a jsem.

Health

I feel dizzy.	**Mám závrať.**
I cannot eat.	**Nemohu jíst.**
I cannot sleep.	**Nemohu spát.**
I feel better.	**Cítim se lépe.**
I feel worse.	**Cítim se hůře.**
I am tired.	**Jsem uneven/á.**
I am pregnant.	**Jsem těhotná.**
I have a(n)	**Mám ... .**
You have a(n)	**Ty máš ... .**
...allergy	**...alergii**
...fever	**...teplotu**
...cold	**...rýmu**
...diarrhea	**...průjem**
...wound	**...ránu, zranění**

I have a cold.
Jsem nachlazen/a.

I am allergic to ... .
Jsem alergický/á na ... .
Mám alegrii na ... .

Take these pills once/twice a day.
Berte ty prášky/tablety jednou/dvakrát denně.

You will be fine.
Budete se cítit lepé.

I have	**Bolí mě ... .**
...a backache	**...záda**
...an earache	**...ucho**
...a headache	**...hlava**
...a sore throat	**...v krku**
...a stomachache	**...žaludek**

I have high blood pressure.
Mám vysoký krevní tlak.

I have low blood pressure.
Mám nízký krevní tlak.

sunstroke	**úžeh, úpal**
food poisoning	**otrava jídlem**
heart attack	**srdeční infarkt,**
	srdeční záchvat
broken bone	**zlomená, rozbitá kost**
sprain	**vyvrtnutí, vymknutí**

At the Dentist

Could you recommend a good dentist?
Můžete mi doporučit dobrého zubaře?

I've lost a filling.
Vypadla mi plomba.

I have a broken tooth.
Zlomil se mi zub.

tooth	**zub**
teeth	**zuby**
toothache	**bolení zubů**

Eyesight

I need glasses.
Potřebuji brýle.

I have broken my glasses.
Zlomil/a jsem si brýle.

Can you repair them, please?
Můžete je, prosím opravit.

optical	**zrakový, optický**
optician	**optik**
eye	**oko**
eyesight	**zrak**

Parts of the Body

ankle	**kotník**
arm	**paže**
back	**záda**
beard	**vousy**
blood	**krev**
body	**tělo**
bone	**kost**
breast	**prsa**
chest	**hruď**
chin	**brada**
ear	**ucho**
elbow	**loket**
face	**obličej**
finger	**prst**
hair	**vlasy**
hand	**ruka**
head	**hlava**
heart	**srdce**
kidney	**ledvina**
knee	**koleno**
leg	**noha**
lip	**ret**
liver	**játra**
lung	**plíce**
mouth	**ústa**

neck	**krk**
nose	**nos**
shoulder	**rameno**
stomach	**žaludek**
throat	**hrdlo**
thumb	**palec**
toe	**prst u nohy**
tongue	**jazyk**
vein	**žíla**

14. WEATHER

What's the weather like today?
Jak je dnes venku?

It's sunny/cloudy.
Je slunečno/zataženo.

It's warm/cool/cold.
Je teplo/chladno/zima.

It's foggy.
Je mlha.

It's raining.
Prší.

It's snowing.
Sněží.

Where is the wind from?
Odkud fouká vítr?

From the north/east/south/west.
Ze severu/východu/jihu/západu.

What's the temperature?
Kolik je stupňů?

thunderstorm	**bouře**
thunderbolt	**bles**
wind	**vítr**
cloud	**mrak**
cloudy weather	**oblačno**
cloudy	**zatažený**
weather	**počasí**
fine weather	**pěkné počasí**

15. TIME

What time is it?	**Kolik je hodin?**
It's 9 A.M.	**V 9. (devět)**
	h. (hodin) ráno.
It's 8 P.M.	**V 8. (osm)**
	h. (hodin) večer.
	Ve 20. (dvacet)
	h. (hodin).
Around 8 P.M.	**Kolem 20. (dvacet)**
	h. (hodin) večer.

hour	**hodina**
minute	**minuta**
half	**půl**
half an hour	**půl hodiny**
half past two	**půl třetí**
quarter	**čtvrt**
a quarter of an hour	**čtvrt hodiny**
A.M.	**ráno**
P.M.	**večer**

It is a quarter to six.
Je tříčtvrti na šest.

It is a quarter past five.
Je čtvrt na šest.

It is 7:30 P.M.
Je 7 (sedm) h. (hodin) a 30 (třicet) m. (minut) večer.
Je půl osmé večer. Je 19 (devatenáct) h. (hodin) a 30 (třicet) m. (minut).

It is early.	**Je brzy.**
It is late.	**Je pozdě.**

in the morning	ráno
in the afternoon	odpoledne
in the evening	večer
at midnight	v(o) půlnoci

day	den
today	dnes
yesterday	včera
tomorrow	zítra
the day before yesterday	předevčírem

last night	minulý večer
four days before	před čtyřmi dny
three days before	před třemi dny

two weeks ago	před dvěma týdny
this week	tento týden
last week	minulý týden
next week	příští týden

this month	tento měsíc
last month	minulý měsíc
next month	příští měsíc

this year	tento rok
last year	minulý rok
next year	příští rok

What day is it today?
Který den je dnes?

Today is Friday.
Dnes je pátek.

What day will it be tomorrow?
Který den bude zítra?

this morning	**dnes ráno**
now	**teď**
at the moment	**v tuto chvíli**
tonight	**v noci, dnes večer**
night	**noc**
year	**rok**
month	**měsíc**
week	**týden**
spring	**jaro**
summer	**léto**
autumn	**podzim**
winter	**zima**

Days of the week

Monday	**pondělí**
Tuesday	**úterý**
Wednesday	**středa**
Thursday	**čtvrtek**
Friday	**pátek**
Saturday	**sobota**
Sunday	**neděle**
on Monday	**v pondělí**

Months of the year

January	**leden**
February	**únor**
March	**březen**
April	**duben**
May	**květen**
June	**červen**

July	**červenec**
August	**srpen**
September	**září**
October	**říjen**
November	**listopad**
December	**prosinec**

Holidays

Christmas	**Vánoce**
New Year's, New Year's Eve	**Nový rok, Silvestr**
Easter	**Velikonoce**

16. COLORS

black	**černý**
brown	**hnědý**
blue	**modrý**
green	**zelený**
orange	**oranžový**
red	**červený**
white	**bílý**
yellow	**žlutý**
purple	**červenofialový**

17. NUMBERS

Cardinal

one	**jeden** (M), **jedna** (F), **jedno** (N)
two	**dva, dvě**
three	**tři**
four	**čtyři**
five	**pět**
six	**šest**
seven	**sedm**
eight	**osm**
nine	**devět**
ten	**deset**
eleven	**jedenáct**
twelve	**dvanáct**
thirteen	**třináct**
fourteen	**čtrnáct**
fifteen	**patnáct**
sixteen	**šesnáct**
seventeen	**sedmnáct**
eighteen	**osmnáct**
nineteen	**devatenáct**
twenty	**dvacet**
twenty-one	**dvacet jeden, jedenadvacet**
thirty	**třicet**
forty	**čtyřicet**
fifty	**padesát**
sixty	**šedesát**
seventy	**sedmdesát**
eighty	**osmdesát**
ninety	**devadesát**
hundred	**sto**
two hundred	**dvě stě**
thousand	**tisíc**
two thousand	**dva tisíce**

Ordinal

1st	**první**
2nd	**druhý**
3rd	**třetí**
4th	**čtvrtý**
5th	**pátý**
6th	**šestý**
7th	**sedmý**
8th	**osmý**
9th	**devátý**
10th	**desatý**

18. MEASUREMENTS AND CONVERSION TABLES

Length

1 inch = 2.54 centimeters (cm)
1 cm = 0.39 inches
1 foot = 0.305 meters (m)
1 meter = 3.28 feet
1 yard = 0.91 meters
1 m = 1.09 yards
1 mile = 1.61 kilometer (km)
1 km = 0.62 miles = ⅝ miles

Weight

1 ounce = 28.35 grams (g)
100 g = 3.5 oz
1 pound = 0.45 kilograms (kg)
1 kg = 2.2 lb

Volume

1 U.S. pint = 0.47 liters (1)
1 liter = 2.13 U.S. pints
1 US gallon = 3.79 liters
1 liter = 0.26 U.S. gallons

Measurements and Conversion Tables

Temperature

Fahrenheit (**F**)   Centigrade/Celsius (**C**)

$C = (F - 32) \times 5/9$ $F = (C \times 9/5) + 32$

C	F
−18	0
−12	10
− 7	20
− 1	30
4	40
10	50
15	60
21	70
26	80
31	90
37	100

kilometer	**kilometr**	**(km)**
meter	**metr**	**(m)**
centimeter	**centimetr**	**(cm)**
millimeter	**milimetr**	**(mm)**
kilo	**kilo**	**(k)**
gram	**grame**	**(g)**
kilogram	**kilogram**	**(kg)**
liter	**litr**	**(l)**

REFERENCES

Anglická konverzace. Praha: Rebo production, 2000.

Čornej, P. *Fundamentals of Czech History.* Prague: Práh, 1992.

Kučera, J., a kolektiv. *Kapesní slovník Česko-anglický Anglicko-český.* Olomouc: Nakladatelství Olomouc, 2000.

Machala, L., Petrů, E. *Panorama české literatury.* Olomouc: Rubico, 1994.

Mawadza, A. *Shona-English/English-Shona Dictionary and Phrasebook.* New York: Hippocrene Books, 2000.

Melichar, J., Styblík,V. *Český jazyk.* Praha: SPN, 1974.

Merriam-Webster's Collegiate Dictionary. http://www.m-w.com/cgi-bin/dictionary

Merriam-Webster Dictionary of Synonyms and Antonyms, The. Springfield, Massachusetts: Merriam-Webster, Inc., 1992.

Šára, M., Šarová, J., Bytel, A. *Čeština pro cizince.* Praha: SPN, 1969.

Webster's New World Dictionary. New York: Fawcett Popular Library, 1979.

Webster's New World Thesaurus. New York: Fawcett Popular Library, 1974.

Other Czech Interest Titles from Hippocrene Books . . .

Dictionaries & Language Guides

Czech-English/English-Czech Concise Dictionary
7,500 entries • 598 pages • 4 x 6 • 0-87052-981-1 • $11.95pb • (276)

Czech-English/English-Czech Standard Dictionary,
10th Revised Edition
40,000 entries • 1,072 pages • 6 x 9 • 0-7818-0653-4 • $39.50hc • (740)

Hippocrene Children's Illustrated Czech Dictionary
English-Czech/Czech-English
500 entries • 94 pages • 8½ x 11 • 0-7818-0987-8 • $11.95pb • (579)

Czech Handy Extra Dictionary
2,600 entries • 100 pages • 5 x 7¾ • 0-7818-0138-9 • $8.95pb • (63)

Beginner's Czech
200 pages • 5½ x 8½ • 0-7818-0231-8 • $9.95pb • (74)

Czech Phrasebook
220 pages • 5½ x 8½ • 0-87052-967-6 • $9.95pb • (599)

Literature

Treasury of Czech Love Poems, Quotations & Proverbs
In Czech and English
128 pages • 5 x 7 • 0-7818-0571-6 • $11.95hc • (670)

Folk Tales from Bohemia
98 pages • 5½ x 8¼ • 0-7818-0718-2 • $14.95hc • (786)

Czech, Moravian & Slovak Fairy Tales
243 pages • 5½ x 8½ • 0-7818-0714-X • $14.95hc • (792)

Cuisine

The Best of Czech Cooking, Expanded Edition
406 pages • 5½ x 8½ • 0-7818-0805-7 • $24.95hc • (456)

Prices subject to change without prior notice. **To purchase Hippocrene Books** contact your local bookstore, call (718) 454-2366, or write to: HIPPOCRENE BOOKS, 171 Madison Avenue, New York, NY 10016. Please enclose check or money order, adding $5.00 shipping (UPS) for the first book, and $.50 for each additional book.